The biopolitics of

Manchester University Press

Simon Tormey and Jon Simons · series editors

The times we live in are troubling, and as always theory struggles to keep pace with events in its efforts to analyse and assess society, culture and politics. Many of the 'contemporary' political theories emerged and developed in the twentieth century or earlier, but how well do they work at the start of the twenty-first century?

Reappraising the Political realigns political theory with its contemporary context. The series is interdisciplinary in approach, seeking new inspiration from both traditional sister disciplines, and from more recent neighbours such as literary theory and cultural studies. It encompasses an international range, recognising both the diffusion and adaptation of Western political thought in the rest of the world, and the impact of global processes and non-Western ideas on Western politics.

already published

Rethinking equality: the challenge of equal citizenship
Chris Armstrong

Radical democracy: politics between abundance and lack
Lars Tønder and Lasse Thomassen (eds)

The biopolitics of the war on terror: life struggles, liberal modernity and the defence of logistical societies
Julian Reid

Time and world politics: thinking the present
Kimberly Hutchings

Unstable universalities: post structuralism and radical politics
Saul Newman

Julian Reid

THE BIOPOLITICS
OF THE WAR ON TERROR

Life struggles, liberal modernity,
and the defence of logistical societies

Manchester University Press

Manchester and New York

distributed in the United States exclusively by Palgrave Macmillan

Copyright © Julian Reid 2006

The right of Julian Reid to be identified as the author
of this work has been asserted by him in accordance with
the Copyright, Designs and Patents Act 1988.

Published by Manchester University Press
Oxford Road, Manchester M13 9NR, UK
and Room 400, 175 Fifth Avenue, New York, NY 10010, USA
www.manchesteruniversitypress.co.uk

Distributed in the United States exclusively by
Palgrave Macmillan, 175 Fifth Avenue,
New York, NY 10010, USA

Distributed in Canada exclusively by
UBC Press, University of British Columbia, 2029 West Mall,
Vancouver, BC, Canada V6T 1Z2

British Library Cataloguing-in-Publication Data is available

Library of Congress Cataloging-in-Publication Data is available

ISBN 978 0 7190 7406 6 paperback

First published in hardback 2006
First published in paperback 2009

The publisher has no responsibility for the persistence or accuracy of URLs
for any external or third-party internet websites referred to in this book,
and does not guarantee that any content on such websites is, or will remain,
accurate or appropriate.

Printed by the MPG Books Group in the UK

The art of war deals with living and with moral forces.

Carl von Clausewitz, *On War*

Contents

Preface and acknowledgements

The War on Terror is currently represented in International Relations and beyond as a conflict between political and social formations for which the security and promotion of human life is an abiding concern and an enemy dedicated to the destruction of the political and social conditions for the flourishing of human life. Not simply an enemy that is motivated against the interests of common humanity, but an enemy which in being so driven, is ready to resort to subhuman tactics, and which therefore requires, paradoxically, a less than human response in defence of the integrity of human life. Hence the declaration by liberal regimes and the mobilisation of their societies for a war of fundamentally illiberal proportions and dimensions. A war deemed to require the permanent mobilisation of entire societies against an enemy which threatens their security from within. A war against an enemy which like a parasite living off its human host, breeds in the most vulnerable areas of liberal societies, waiting for the moment to release a pathological violence upon its otherwise oblivious prey. A war which requires the development of new and evermore intensive techniques with which to monitor the movements and dispositions of the life of liberal societies themselves because it is there that the enemy festers and will emerge to such devastating effect.

To challenge such broadly disseminated understandings this book develops a biopolitical analysis of the War on Terror. Examining this war biopolitically means attempting to think more rigorously about the actuality of relations between the problems of life and politics which are constitutive of it. In developing this analysis it is especially important that we subject to critique the claim firstly that liberal regimes do indeed exist for the security and promotion of human life, and secondly that the terrorists now targeting liberal societies are themselves devoid of human causes and aspirations. In essence, and as will be argued, this is not a war in defence of the integrity of human life against an enemy defined simply by a contradictory will for the destruction of human life. It is a war over the political constitution of life in which the limitations of liberal accounts of humanity are being put to the test, if not rejected outright. It is certainly true that the future of humanity is at stake in this conflict, but only in the sense that any resolution of it will depend on our abilities to learn to question the limits of existing understandings of what constitutes human life and its political potentialities. The instigation of such a line of questioning is integral to the biopolitical analysis developed in this book.

As a struggle over the political constitution of life this war entails a substantial genealogy. It can be traced back, at the very least, to the origins of liberal regimes, which from their inception in the seventeenth and eighteenth centuries have sought to govern life with a view to the elimination of the problem of war from within and between societies. The development of the liberal project of peace has, of course, met with serial resistances throughout modernity. Yet the end of the Cold War and the fall of the Soviet Union led many to declare that its central aims had been fulfilled. Today, in the context of the War on Terror, the original dilemmas of liberal modernity are being posed anew and in evermore forceful terms. Why is it that a political project dedicated to solving the problem of war and the creation of peace has culminated in the declaration of a war bereft of temporal or spatial parameters? Why is it that a political project which seeks to sever the relation of society to war now requires a social state of permanent mobilisation for war? What accounts for the ferocity with which human societies and subjects attempt to protect accounts of life inimical to liberal conditions? What is to be done about such obvious and immediate failings of liberalism to convince life to submit itself to humanist dominions?

Responding to these dilemmas requires not only that we analyse the ways in which liberal regimes have sought and failed historically to martial life in the interests of liberal peace, but that we pose anew the problem of what life is and may become once released from the shackles that liberal regimes attempt to bind it with in the name of peace. As this book argues, it is our failing to establish the political grounds from which to pursue meaningful responses to such urgent problems that accounts currently for the prevalence of the form of resistance to the liberal project known as Terror.

This book examines these problems through the development of a conceptual framework derived from the works of a group of thinkers uniquely provisioned for such a task. Indeed the formulation of the problem of relations between war, life, and politics on which the analysis turns would not be possible without them. The works of Michel Foucault and other major political and social thinkers influenced by him are among the most under-utilised and yet over-abused resources of International Relations theory. Work within International Relations influenced by Foucault has generally been accused of irrelevance to disciplinary concerns. In this book I explain the critical importance of Foucault for a problem that is absolutely central to the discipline of International Relations. That is the problem of war and the political mechanisms through which societies have attempted to mitigate it. Through Foucault it is possible to pose questions and develop modes of analysis of the relations between war and the development of liberal societies that take us some way beyond the ordinary limits of studies derived from existing traditions of IR. Indeed, traditional theories of International Relations are in the process found to be constitutive of the very problems of war and its relations to the development of liberal modernity which International Relations is tasked to solve.

Not only is it the case that Foucault's work has been under-utilised in the development of theoretical accounts of problems of war and peace in International Relations; the importance and complexity of the problem of war for the development of liberal modernity has been otherwise neglected in broader areas of social and political theory. Even in the secondary literatures which attempt to cash in on the specificities of Foucauldian accounts of modernity there has been an unwarranted neglect of the centrality of the debate on war to Foucault's work and others influenced by him. This book redresses that neglect by also offering an account of that debate as it has developed between Foucault and other thinkers whose work approximates to his; specifically Gilles Deleuze and Felix Guattari, Jean Baudrillard, Paul Virilio, and latterly Michael Hardt and Antonio Negri.

For many, Foucault's work is associated with the decline in the power of collective political subjects, with an increasingly limited horizon of political possibilities, even with the disenchantment of the political itself. In contrast this book aims to make clear the importance of his work for our capacities to recognise how this crisis came about. How it was that liberal regimes developed the means with which to seize, shape and condition the life of their societies to such depoliticising effect. And, crucially, the importance of his work for our ability to recover the vital capacity to think and act politically in circumstances when, as will be explored in this book, the most basic expressions of thought and human action are being targeted for new techniques of surveillance and governance.

Throughout the tradition of Foucauldian thought explored within this book there recurs a question and problem. Not just that of how to explain the ways in which liberal regimes have failed to overcome the problem of war in the development of their projects of peace in promotion of human life. And certainly not that of how we might better equip liberal regimes with the means to suborn life more fully. But that of how life itself, in its subjection to governance, can and does resist, subvert, escape and defy the imposition of modes of governance which seek to remove it of those very capacities for resistance, subversion, flight, and defiance. In each of the chapters that follow I have sought to delineate the specificities of different accounts of what life is and can become in spite of, and mainly because of, its subjection to techniques of governance which aim at reducing it to states of docility, plasticity and logistical order. As we will see, the formulation of and response to this problem is dealt with differently by each of the Foucauldian thinkers that I engage with in the book. Foucauldian thought is not monolithic and the debates being engaged with here are far from settled.

The bulk of the book itself was written in a summer of immense uncertainty, fear, and unrest. During July 2005 I took pleasure in participating in the mass social protests against the imposition of global liberal regimes of governance which took place in and around the summit of the G8 in Scotland. In spite of the immense evidence for powers of hope and the strength of desires for transformation on display during that week, it was impossible not to be struck, and in a certain sense impressed, by the ease with which the entire event was policed, and by the precision with which the conflict between life and law was mediated and ultimately stifled. In turn, this experience of the densely mediated and subdued forms which much of political action tends to assume today was thrown into stark contrast by the 7 July Terror attacks in London, occurring as they did on the first day of the summit proper. Clearly, there exists today a disjunctive terrain between the political imaginaries and practices of the different adversaries and enemies of liberalism. It is imperative that we traverse that terrain thoughtfully if a more substantial alternative to the liberal way of life is to come about.

The writing of this book in the aftermath of the Terror attacks in London has also been an unsettling experience. The fashioning of new laws dedicated to the diminishment of freedoms of political thought and expression within the United Kingdom, and the threat of draconian punishments for those who are declared to break those laws, is inevitably making the task of political critique that much more precarious. In an earlier era Foucault himself described the task of the practice of criticism as that of 'a matter of making facile gestures difficult'. Today, in contrast it might be said, the task is the recovery and defence of the art of critique in the context of regimes against which the most facile gesture is made at risk of being sequestered as a source of insecurity and threat.

Although much of this book was written over the summer of 2005, the ideas that feed it, and the earlier research works that inform it, have a longer history. The basic idea of developing a Foucauldian account of the problem of war and its relation to liberal modernity began with the writing of a PhD thesis under the supervision of Michael Dillon. To him I am profoundly grateful for his unruly governance. Without his encouragement and faith the project would doubtless have assumed a different and more limited form. I am also grateful to David Campbell and Scott Wilson for their comments and suggestions on the thesis manuscript which helped give the project a new impetus in the process of deciding how to transform it into a book.

Most of the chapters which make up the book began life as research articles written towards the end of or shortly after the thesis. Each in turn has been substantially altered and shaped as it has been made to discover its calling as part of a greater whole. The first chapter draws in part on my article 'War, Liberalism and Modernity: The Biopolitical Provocations of *Empire*' in the *Cambridge Review of International Affairs* (volume 17, number 1, April 2004), 63–79. The second chapter is informed in part by 'Life Struggles: War, Discipline and Biopolitics in the Thought of Michel Foucault' in *Social Text* (volume 86, Spring 2006), 127–52. The third chapter draws on 'The Biopolitics of the War on Terror: A Critique of the Return of Imperialism Thesis in International Relations' in *Third World Quarterly* (volume 26, number 2, 2005), 237–52. And the fifth chapter developed originally as 'Architecture, Al Qaeda, and the World

Preface and acknowledgements

Trade Center: Rethinking Relations between War, Modernity and City Spaces after 9/11' in *Space and Culture* (volume 7, number 4, November 2004), 396–408. Early drafts of each of these chapters were also presented at British International Studies Association conferences at the University of Birmingham and at the University of Warwick; the Security Bytes conference at Lancaster University; the International Studies Association conference in Montreal; the Cities as Strategic Sites Conference in Manchester; the Centre for Rights, Justice, Violence and War Seminar Series at Sussex University; the Centre for the Study of Democracy Seminar Series at the University of Westminster; a European Liberty and International Security workshop in Montreal; the Political Studies Department workshop on International Politics at the School of Oriental and African Studies, London; the International Security and Global Governance workshop on Security and Violence in the Contemporary Age at Birkbeck College. I thank the organisers of those events for inviting me to talk as well as the participants for their comments. Particular thanks are due to Claudia Aradau, Benjamin Arditi, Tarak Barkawi, Shane Brighton, Dave Chandler, Martin Coward, Patrick Deer, Stefan Elbe, Michael Hardt, Laura Junka, Mark Laffey, Matteo Mandarini, Randy Martin, Andrew Neal, Louiza Odysseos, Andrew Schaap, Jeremy Valentine, and Rob Walker, for commenting on early drafts of these works. None of them, that said, should be held responsible for the arguments and analysis made here.

I am indebted also to the students who sat in on my graduate course 'War, Power and Modern Societies: Foucauldian Perspectives' which I taught at the University of Sussex in the spring of 2005. The conversations and debates generated by the seminars were tremendously helpful when it came to sitting down and writing the text. Sussex provided me with a near to ideal intellectual environment in which to write this book, and I am grateful to all who engaged me during my time there. Particular thanks to Joel Duncan and Ben Trott for their camaraderie over the summer.

I am very grateful to the editors of the 'Reappraising the Political' series, Jon Simons and Simon Tormey, whose advice, encouragement and support has meant very much to me, and whose detailed comments on the manuscript helped tremendously in its revision. Thanks also to the team at Manchester University Press for all their help in preparing the manuscript for publication.

Thanks also to the many others with whom I have shared friendships over the last year. Particular thanks to the artist Keith Farquhar, who is a great friend, and also a unique interlocutor and collaborator. Parts of our work 'Immanent War, Immaterial Terror . . .', *Culture Machine* (2005), also finds its way into this text at various points, it being a condensed expression of the central argument of the book. The work also exhibited as part of Keith's show at NYEHAUS in New York in the autumn of 2005.

Julian Reid, *London*

War and liberal modernity: a biopolitical critique

WITNESSED from the vantage point of a twenty-first century characterised by the apparent pacification and interdependence of societies
globally, liberalism would look to have proven itself the most authoritative
account of the development of modern international relations. Definitive of
liberalism has been its belief in the ability to establish societies through the
removal of life from the condition of war and the provision of political means
to allow human beings to flourish peacefully. From the Hobbesian conception
of a society removed from the condition of war by a sovereign state, to the
Kantian conception of societies gradually overcoming war internationally
through the mitigation of state sovereignty, liberalism has been defined politically by its investment in that ideal as a foundation for the conceptualisation and
development of modernity. Despite the different ways in which political
philosophers as diverse as Kant and Hobbes formulated the problems of war and
peace and despite mistaken claims as to their ideological bipolarity, their works
have converged powerfully in the development of strategies with which to establish peaceful conditions for human life socially. In the transition from the
strategies of pacification with which territorial states first set about the removal
of war from particular societies to the strategies with which global liberal
regimes are now attempting to establish conditions for peaceful living on a planetary scale, the liberal project has gathered pace. The liberal ideal of a society
removed from the condition of war, in the name of an end to all violence, and
in promotion of the welfare of common humanity, has proven to be among the
most alluring of all political horizons sighted in the modern era.

Modernity is obviously a complex concept, referring to diverse processes,
practices, institutions, imperatives, and forms of organisation. To speak of
liberal modernity is not to presume that these conjugated terms are simply
coterminous, nor that liberal modernity is not itself a contested and variable
concept. There exist capitalist modernities, as well as socialist, revolutionary,

and fascist modernities, none of which can be understood as singular, and the development of each of which has been and continues to be inextricably related to many of the processes, practices and institutions which liberal modernity itself partakes of. If modernity comprises the advent of, orientation toward, and struggle of human life for numerous conflicting horizons, then modernity can be said to be divided by definition accordingly. For capitalist modernity the horizon of human life is still powerfully that of profit. For revolutionary modernity it is freedom. For socialist modernity it is equality, and for fascist modernity the horizon of life is power. It is obvious that none of these horizons are exclusively capitalist, revolutionary, socialist or fascist, just as it would be absurd to argue that the horizon of peace is exclusively liberal. Liberal modernity orients itself so as to allow for the production of a measured sensibility among living human creatures in which the experience and love of power, freedom, equality, and of profit may commingle, just as fascist modernity lays claim to its own forms of freedom, profit, and equality. Indeed this is precisely why the relations between liberalism and fascism are so unstable. But we can still speak of the specificity of a particular modernity in which the orientation and movement of human life toward various horizons is precluded by the fixity with which one ideal governs and rules all relations with modernity's other variable forms. In this sense the concept of liberal modernity captures the processes in and through which the international development of human practices, institutions, and forms of organisation has been shaped by the governance of the ideal of peace to the detriment of other possible mutations.

If liberal modernity has been shaped most powerfully by the ideal of peace, it has nevertheless been defined in epochal terms not only by the recurrence of war, but by a gradual increase in military capacities among liberal societies for the violent destruction of human life. Not simply the increasingly industrial scale of military massacres during the nineteenth and early twentieth centuries, nor the absurdities of strategies of mutually assured destruction during the late twentieth century, but the establishment of new biotechnological capacities for the targeting of life during the twenty-first century, remind us of the ultimately paradoxical character of liberal modernity. A political project based concretely on the ideal of peace in the service of humanity has continually served to reinvent and bolster its nemesis, war. Not only has the recurrence of war throughout modernity served to underline its paradoxical character, but the increasing precision with which human life is targeted for killing in war, severely undermines the foundations of the project of liberal modernity understood in terms of the pursuit of sustainable peace. No irony, then, in the fact that the inscription on the Dutch innkeeper's door from which Kant borrowed the title to his seminal tract 'Perpetual Peace' appeared above the picture of a graveyard (Kant 1983: 106).

Remarkably, the perspicuity of this paradoxical feature of liberal modernity has done little to deter liberals of the present from continuing to claim the ability to promote peace in the interests of humanity. The advocates of liberal international theory, a tradition which claims a lineage reaching back at least as far as Kant, have continued to argue for, as well as seek, the development of liberal institutions and practices globally (Macmillan 1998; Doyle 1997; Russett 1993; Fukuyama 1992; Doyle 1986; Doyle 1983). They do so, of course, in the faith that the persistent shadow cast upon modernity by war has little bearing upon the actual strength of their social and political frameworks for the provision of peace. And they are reluctant to recognise any link between their own wilful attempts to secure the conditions for the expansion of liberal accounts of human life globally in the name of peace, the recurrence of war, and the newfound capacities among liberal regimes for the destruction of life technologically. The fact especially, that in spite of the apparent pacific qualities of liberal societies, relations between liberal and illiberal societies have been and continue to be defined by war, has done little to deter the essential faith of liberals in their project. Indeed the recurring tendencies of liberal regimes to wage war upon illiberal societies has been explained and justified as a problematic but ultimately acceptable corollary of the expansion of the zone of liberal peace (Fukuyama 1992: 263–4). In spite of its failings, liberalism remains for its foremost proponents, 'an extraordinary beacon of hope' (Doyle 1997: 480).

In response to the attacks of 11 September 2001, the United States and other liberal regimes allied to it, including the United Kingdom, have declared a new form of war, a War on Terror. The form of this war is unprecedented in its breadth and intensity. Declaring war against an enemy which, as the President of the United States, George W. Bush, has described, lacks 'great armies and great industrial capabilities', has no 'nation or citizens to defend', and which exists 'hidden in caves and growing in laboratories' (Freedman 2002: 40), means that liberal regimes have now committed to a war without end, temporally, spatially, and politically. Three centuries after Kant's pronouncement of the ways in which liberal practices and institutions would gradually emancipate humanity from the condition of war, liberal societies find themselves entering a new stage of development requiring their permanent mobilisation against an enemy said to move in unforeseeable ways, which strikes at unforeseeable times, festering in the hidden recesses of their own dense infrastructures. International Relations (IR) is *the* discipline uniquely tasked with the provision of understandings and explanations for such major paradoxes of war and peace. Yet it is failing us in this important respect. As a discipline it has been and continues to be profoundly shaped by the influence of ideas drawn precisely from the tradition of thought and practice responsible for the generation of this paradox, liberalism. The essence of the 'democratic peace' thesis, the contemporary form of Kant's original argument, remains alive and well within the discipline, celebrated even by the claim that the 'absence of war between democracies comes as

[3]

close as anything we have to an empirical law in international relations' (Levy 1988: 662). The exacerbation of the problem of war between liberal and illiberal regimes continues to be treated as some kind of resistant remnant of a declining anti-modernity, some virulent but ultimately treatable pathology of a global system that is gradually being reshaped in the interests of peace for humanity. Moreover, the depth and intensity with which the condition of war now affects the ordinary existence of life within liberal societies, the logistical and security imperatives newly shaping and conditioning the liberal way of life, is incomprehensible to a discipline that continues to function with the limited conception of war as an act of combat between the regular armed forces of nation-states (Black 2004: 119–62; Hirst 2001: 79–109).

This is not to say that liberalism does not already possess its critics in the study of international relations. The failings of liberal modernity to realise its pacific ends have become, over the years, increasingly well documented through the development of critical literatures on international relations. Indeed, the very definition of liberalism as a body of thought and practice dedicated toward the establishment of peace has been increasingly challenged by accounts of the function of war as a perennial instrument for the power-seeking strategies of liberal regimes (Barkawi 2006; Barkawi and Laffey 2001; Barkawi and Laffey 1999). Following the end of the Cold War and the subsequent proliferation of the phenomenon of so-called 'humanitarian war', such critiques have developed at pace. In response to the many attempts of liberal regimes to represent their use of war in the post-Cold War era as humanitarian and subordinate to the cause of peace, a slew of critics have sought to reveal the strategic imperatives motivating liberal regimes. Danilo Zolo, for example, has argued the attempts of liberal regimes to qualify their use of war as 'humanitarian' 'to be a typical ploy for self-legitimisation ... part and parcel of war itself, an instrument of military strategy in the strict sense, used to obtain victory over the enemy' (2002: 38). David Chandler, in a slightly different fashion, has denounced the humanitarian agenda of liberal regimes as 'a narcissistic one, not concerned with external change to develop the rights and freedoms for people across the world, but with domestic angst about a fragmenting society' (2002: 226). The advent of the War on Terror, and the subsequent military invasion and political and economic colonisation of Afghanistan and Iraq, has lent new vigour to such lines of critique. Authors such as Ellen Meiksens Wood argue that the continuing attempts of the foremost liberal regime, the United States, to claim allegiance to the interests of peace and humanitarian values serves only to conceal 'underlying principles of US global hegemony and military supremacy' (Wood 2005: 162). As such, the claim of liberal regimes to the promotion of peace is, it has been frequently argued, an ideological fiction, and the faith of liberals in their abilities to promote the rights of humanity a matter of sheer hypocrisy.

This book will pursue a different line of critique against liberal claims to the promotion of peace and the welfare of humanity. It is insufficient when attempting to comprehend the nature of the relations between liberal regimes and war, to dismiss their commitments to the promotion of peace and the ideal of a common humanity simply as rhetorical devices for the disguise of ulterior, largely materially driven, strategic motivations. Such lines of critique, as popular as they currently are, do not even scratch the surface of the problem of relations between war and the power dynamics of liberal regimes and their societies. Rather, if we want to unravel the paradoxical relations of liberal regimes to war, we have to address the ways in which the development of the problem of war among liberal regimes has been shaped and conditioned profoundly by the limits of their conceptualisations of peace and humanity. Liberal ideals of what constitutes a peaceful society, what forms of life are compatible with the existence of liberal peace, and are thus deemed worthy of the title of human, have developed through a state of continual antagonism, or what one author once described as a state of 'more or less veiled civil war' (Marx 1988: 66), with rival life-forms. The historical development and planetary expansion of liberal regimes has been inextricably tied to their capacities not simply to represent themselves as promoters of the well-being of humanity, but to command and control prevailing conceptions of what constitutes the well-being of human life; its definitive needs, interests and desires. It is disappointing that in their attempts to expose liberal regimes' discourses of peace and humanity as hypocrisy, authors such as Zolo, Wood and Chandler opt to leave the question of the authenticity of liberal accounts of *what human life is* and *what human life may become* untouched. If anything, such lines of critique have only served to re-enforce the veracity of liberal accounts of the limits and potentialities of human life because they rest upon the crudity of a distinction between strategic and human motivations. Their critiques are not aimed in any sense at exposing the political, ethical or social limitations of the ideas of humanity and peace which inform the motivations of liberal regimes, but merely at questioning their use (Zolo 2002: 39). In turn they are based upon the errant supposition of the moral restitution of the ideal of a permanent state of peace in the interests of common humanity in a world rid of the regimes said to be instrumentally abusing it (Chandler 2002: 236).

Addressing the failings of the liberal project to secure peaceful conditions for the sustenance of humanity requires, instead, that we be highly suspicious not simply of the use which liberal regimes make of ideas of peace and humanity, but of the content of these concepts in and of themselves. We have to pose the question of why, when and how it was that human life came to be so conceived. Which forms of life have been and are deemed capable of peaceful living under liberal conditions and, conversely, which forms are associated with the threat of war? In responding to these questions we have to examine liberal regimes, as Michel Foucault urged us to, *biopolitically*. This book does precisely that by tracing the development of liberal regimes back to the origins of their emergence in the eighteenth century and the development of the techniques with which they first set out to posit a solution to the problem of war through the pacification of life and the imposition of liberal accounts of humanity within their own and other societies. It was in that particular period that liberal regimes first discovered the means by which to seize and manipulate the life of their societies in hitherto unprecedented ways. The modern project of solving the problem of war, of eliminating the phenomenon of violence from within and between societies by exercising power over life directly, has entailed the most profound implications for the ways in which the definition of human life, its essential needs, interests and desires has been conceptualised within liberal societies themselves. The fact that existing and conventional critiques of liberal regimes merely replicate such conceptions of peace and humanity is very much a measure of that influence.

In order to examine liberal regimes biopolitically this book develops, therefore, an overtly Foucauldian analysis. It is only with recourse to the work of Foucault and other specific thinkers influenced by him that we can reveal the embodiment of the liberal account of life in the context of the ways in which liberal regimes have sought to resolve the problem of war. Liberal regimes have not merely sought to use war as an instrument in their strategies of material aggrandisement and territorial expansion. Their entire frameworks of social organisation and human conduct have been radically shaped by their fear for forms of life believed to be inimical to the conditions of their frameworks for the establishment of peace. This is not a problem of a hypocrisy that must be revealed and exposed; it is closer to the problem of a pathology the origins and development of which must be traced and diagnosed. In view of this end, Foucault's own work is of unrivalled importance. For it is in his work specifically that the problems of war, life, and the development of liberal modernity were first articulated in such a way.

Foucault, war, and International Relations

It is remarkable, to say the least, that Foucault's work has enjoyed nothing more than a subsidiary influence upon the development of the theorisation of the problem of war in International Relations to date. If one looks to the major theoretical works written on war and peace in International Relations in recent years one finds scant, if any, reference to his ideas. Thus a book such as Kalevi J. Holsti's *The State, War, and the State of War* (2001), a work which, as its title suggests, claims a thorough theory of the relationship between war and the modern state, makes no mention of Foucault. Sandra Halperin's *War and Social Change in Modern Europe* (2004), a text which claims to theorise the conjunction of changing forms of war and society in the modern era, completely ignores

Foucault's interventions in this particular debate, as does Mary Kaldor's *Old and New Wars* (2002); recent works by the otherwise insightful Martin Shaw on *War & Genocide* (2003) and *The New Western Way of War* do likewise (2005). Even as exhaustive a text as Philip Bobbitt's recent *The Shield of Achilles: War, Peace and the Course of History* (2003), a work which claims to offer all the major answers to the burning questions of war and peace in the modern era, makes no mention of Foucault's theories. If we look to the broader areas of social and political theory where Foucault's work has found more immediate and receptive constituencies one finds, in spite of occasional exceptions (Pick 1993; Dandeker 1990), little discussion of the profound implications of his work for the under-standing of relations of war to the social and political development of liberal modernity. Thus Anthony Giddens' widely regarded attempt to theorise the relationship between modernity and violence in social and political contexts offers only the most superficial of engagements with Foucault's own theorisa-tion of this relation. Indeed Giddens completely ignores the specificity of Foucault's arguments on relations between war and the development of disci-plinary power in his account of the latter's function in the organisation of modern capitalist societies (2002: 182–5).

Since the early 1990s, however, Foucault's work can be seen to have made a gradual impact upon the development of what have unsatisfactorily been described as 'post-structuralist' theories of International Relations (Edkins 1999; Campbell 1998). This in spite of the fact that Foucault himself never saw fit to recognise this term as a relevant or fitting description of the parameters of his work (1997a: 437–48). In spite of the relative attraction which Foucault's work now holds for some International Relations theorists, the specificity of his arguments on the problem of war has, surprisingly, been given little attention. Even in dedicated attempts to describe the importance of Foucault for the study of International Relations his arguments on war have as often been ignored in favour of the rehashing of his accounts of the Panopticon and the emergence of the nineteenth-century prison system as models for the development of disci-plinary practices (Edkins 1999: 41–63). These are not by any means unimportant aspects of Foucault's work. But they are topics which have already been discussed at length in broader areas of social and political theory. Clearly they are not topics integral to the traditional tasking of International Relations in the way that the problem of war is, and their implications for the theorisation of International Relations have often been insufficiently explained. In the context of these failings it is not surprising that the discipline of International Relations has been able to retain a degree of resistance to research influenced by Foucault.

That said there are some important precursors in International Relations to the arguments to be deployed here. The development of the work of David Campbell and Michael Dillon during the 1990s has led to major changes in the ways that traditional problems, if not of war specifically, then at least of security, foreign policy and identity, are theorised in the discipline. And this is due not least to the seminal influence that Foucault has exerted upon these two pre-eminent theorists of International Relations. Campbell's major work, *Writing Security,* first published in 1992, drew on Foucault to interrogate the problem of security biopolitically. As Campbell argued, security is not, as International Relations theorists have traditionally purported (for example Walt 1991), an objective condition which can be specified scientifically and which states then seek to provide to the universal benefit of the life and well-being of their citizens through methods of territorial defence. Security is, first and foremost, a *discursive practice* through which states demarcate what Campbell describes as the 'ethical boundaries of identity' (1998: 200) between forms of life deemed normal, civilised and worthy of inclusion within society, and forms of life deemed abnormal, barbaric and dangerous, and which in being so are deemed to pose a threat to the constitution of the life of society. As such security is a practice which serves the function of reinforcing the power of political regimes over the potential for life of their own society for it is a practice which targets that life directly, imposing limits through which such potentiality is given expression (1998: 199–201). The problem of security is always posed internally at those who live within the society being secured as much as it is posed at others living beyond the territorial boundaries of regimes claiming the capacity to provide security.

To prove this, Campbell focused empirically on the ways in which the discourses of security which have distinguished the foreign policies of modern states, and most especially the United States, have functioned historically to enable their control over the constitution of life within domestic societies. For example, during the Cold War, the United States developed a foreign policy involving the discursive depiction of the threat of the way of life known as 'communism' to the well-being of American society. As Campbell demonstrated, the implications of this discourse were as much concerned with policing life within American society as with protecting the territorial boundaries of the state. The representation of the threat of communism in US foreign policy was connoted discursively in a way that generated fears within American society for individuals and populations, the danger of whom was defined by dint simply of their racial, sexual, gendered or class-based difference (Campbell 1998: 133–68). As such, the discursive commitment to securing the United States from the threat of communism created new boundaries between forms of life deemed compatible with the security of American society and forms of life deemed threatening to American society. In turn, the control of the United States over the boundary of identity was bolstered, aiding and abetting the development of biopolitical techniques with which to enforce the demarcation between normal and abnormal modes of social life, and in turn shape the dispositions of subjects.

War and liberal modernity

The groundwork for Campbell's seminal account of the problematic relationships between security and identity can be found partly in the earlier works
of Michael Dillon. Dillon's developing interrogation of the problem of security
through Foucault dates back to the late 1980s, and it was partly his redefinition
of security as political practice as opposed to objective condition which inspired
Campbell's more extensive treatment of the topic (Dillon 1990; Dillon 1989). In
the later period of the 1990s Dillon made as substantial a contribution to the
development of a Foucauldian treatment of the problem of security with the
publication of his *Politics of Security*. There, he drew further on Foucault to
move the biopolitical critique of the problem of security in International
Relations into another dimension. In contrast to Campbell's empirical method
of documenting the ways in which states construct and enforce boundaries
between forms of life deemed normal, civilised and worthy of securing, and
those forms of life deemed fearful and dangerous, Dillon mounted a direct
attack on the ontological account of human life as that form of life distinguished
by its *being insecure* and *in need of security* upon which the sovereignty of all
modern political regimes, he claimed, have been founded. The central question
he posed through Foucault was not that of how political regimes such as the
nation-state have sought to draw the boundary between forms of life to be
secured and forms of life which threaten security, but that of how it was 'that
seeking security became such an insistent and relentless (inter)national preoccupation for humankind?' (1996: 15). As Dillon argued, the problem which
Foucault allows us to pose is not simply that of how political regimes go about
enforcing their power over life through the demarcation of boundaries between
secure and insecure forms of subjectivity, but how it was that this preoccupation
with security first came about. For this preoccupation with security, he argued
convincingly, precedes and exceeds the existence of states by some measure.
Indeed, the ways in which regimes have dealt with the problem of security in
international relations he argued cannot be comprehended without encountering the ways in which the problem of security has invested the entire tradition
of modern political thought on which such regimes are founded. As such, Dillon
argued, if we are to get to the bottom of the problem of the ways in which
modern forms of political regime wield power over the life of their societies
through the development of security practices, we have to start by questioning
the ontological account of *insecure life* which underwrites their claims as to the
needs of their societies for security. And, in turn, against the conventional
account of human life as that form of life which being insecure requires securing, and which has, as he argues, informed the development of modern political
theory from its inception (1996: 12–35), Dillon urged upon International
Relations the radical task of how to think life outside of or beyond its traditional
preoccupations with security. What forms does life take when, he asked, security is no longer conceived as its *raison d'être* but its *bête noir*?

Together, Campbell and Dillon's works provided a powerful platform from which we should have seen, by now, the development of a more all-encompassing Foucauldian approach to the most pressing issues of international relations in the twenty-first century. To a certain extent the power of their influence is attested to in the reshaping that has occurred of the traditionally policy-oriented sub-disciplines of security and strategic studies in recent years. This shift can be recognised in the relative surge of research occurring under the rubric of what is now known as 'critical security studies' (Wyn Jones 1999; Krause and Williams 1996; Lipschutz 1995). For the mainstay of its existence the study of security in International Relations has revolved around questions of how knowledge can best be garnered to serve the unreflectively presupposed needs of the state or other forms of political regime for security. Indeed this remains a definitive feature of the production of knowledge concerning security in International Relations. In the development of critical security studies, on the other hand, new forms of scholarship are emerging which seek as a matter of course to critique this conventional function of knowledge concerning security in relation to the state, and to develop contrary forms of knowledge dedicated to the service of alternative needs. For example, in the twenty-first century, there is now an increasing amount of work within International Relations dedicated to the promotion of what is described as 'human security' (King and Murray 2001/2002; Axworthy 2001; McRae and Hubert 2001).

Yet this is a concept the genealogy of which extends back, at the very least, into the period of the Cold War when, consequent upon the Helsinki Accord of 1975, liberal regimes began to urge and proclaim a newfound responsibility to the security of a common humanity over and against traditional norms of state sovereignty (Kaldor 2003: 61). As such the development of discourses of human security in displacement of traditional conceptions of state security in International Relations was long prefigured by shifts occurring at the policy level, in the development of new institutions and arrangements of global governance. Indeed, the development of these institutions and parallel discursive commitments to the security of the individual and human rights more generally is part of a set of processes which, from a more authentically Foucauldian perspective, must be regarded with some suspicion (Dillon and Reid 2001; Dillon and Reid 2000). It is a failure, in fact, that in the development of so-called 'critical security studies' this shift has not been met with greater circumspection. In the context of the current War on Terror we can witness these discourses of 'human security' being mobilised to newly embellish the claims to legitimacy of liberal regimes now dedicated to waging war in immediate destruction of human life globally. At the time of writing, the War in Iraq which the US and its allies committed to in the wake of 9/11 has, it is estimated, entailed the death of as many as 43,000 Iraqi civilians. And if we look at the broader shift in the treatment of individual human beings suspected of being involved with the new enemy of Terror we confront unprecedented forms of inhumane treatment being meted out by liberal regimes: the indefinite detention of suspects and the use of torture now being established practices of liberal regimes concerned with the waging of war against Terror (Cole 2003).

The advent of the War on Terror, replete with its generative discourse of titanic struggle between humanity and its inhuman other, demands an explicitly Foucauldian intervention. The claim of the leaders of liberal regimes, such as President Bush of the United States, that it is 'our way of life' and 'our freedom' that is at stake in this new form of conflict (Bush 2001a), and yet that the defence of that way of life requires not only the suspension but abrogation of the basic freedoms supposedly so definitive of liberal living, are sufficient provocation in themselves for such an approach. 'What might be called a society's threshold of modernity has been reached when the life of the species is wagered on its own political strategies' warned Foucault in his final substantial written work. 'For millennia, man remained what he was for Aristotle: a living animal with the additional capacity for a political existence: modern man is an animal whose politics places his existence as a living being in question' (1990: 143).

When Foucault penned these words in the 1970s they were intended to underline the modern paradoxes of the 'atomic situation' then dominating the cartographies of international politics (1990: 137). Currently, with that particular threat displaced, it would seem, by the exigencies of Terror, that we should be no less attentive to the importance of his observations as to the paradoxical status of relations between war and life in the development of modernity. In the Cold War era the grand strategies of hegemonic states such as the United States, the Soviet Union, and other Western European powers were defined by a willingness to wager the life of entire populations upon their abilities to build superior nuclear destructive capacities relative to each other. The means with which they pursued goals of peace and security entailed the subjection of the life of their societies to the possibility of total annihilation in the event of war. In the current era of Terror the political strategies of liberal regimes remain predicated upon the subjection of the life of populations to war, but in new and more insidious ways.

Liberal regimes have made clear, in the context of what they proclaim to be the threats to their ways of life posed by Terror, their willingness to wager on their abilities to suborn the life of their enemy to the superiority of the forms of peace and humanity on which their own ways of life are founded. The military interventions in Afghanistan and Iraq are only the coarse shell of what leading liberal thinkers are today proclaiming a 'mental war' (Berman 2003: 154–210) for the life of those illiberal peoples currently contesting the imposition of liberal order. If, for Foucault writing in the 1970s, modern man was an animal whose political strategies placed his existence as a living being in question because he was willing to gamble on the possibility of absolute destruction in pursuit of his security, so in the twenty-first century liberal humanity is a being whose security is threatened by its refusal to question the veracity of its distinction between what does and does not constitute a life worth living. In turn, the strategies of liberal regimes being deployed today in the attempt to transform the life of those societies where Terror is said to harbour, are directly predicated on the martial techniques with which the life of fully-functioning liberal societies was once sequestered. The liberal way of life, which the leaders of liberal regimes as well as the proponents of liberal international theory, proclaim as the progenitor of peace, has its ultimate origins in the preparation of societies for the act of war. This is a fundamental insight to be derived from Foucault, and fully explored in this book, which has never substantially been addressed or considered by International Relations theorists concerned with the modern parameters of problems of war and peace. It is a failing which has occurred at a cost. Incapable of facing up to or revealing the origins of its ways of ordering life in war, the 'placing into question' of what I will account for after Foucault as the 'logistical life' of liberal societies has become, instead, the political calling of Terror.

Structure of the book

So goes the argument of this book. Yet in making it, it will be necessary to go some way beyond Foucault. This is a book not about Foucault, but an examination of the problem of war and its relation to the development of liberal societies wrought through an account of what I call Foucauldian thought. It is a book which assumes a guiding premise to which Foucault's work gives us a novel route of access, that of the origins of the liberal way of life in liberal formulations of the problem of war, but which then interrogates that premise from a variety of different theoretical perspectives and in relation to a variety of different issues with ramifications for how we understand the origins, developments and dilemmas of the War on Terror. Each of the chapters of the book examines the biopolitical dimensions of the War on Terror with recourse to a particular thinker. Chapter 2 details Foucault's own neglected account of the origins of modern forms of disciplinary and biopolitical forms of power in the development of the military sciences of organisation. It draws on Foucault to demonstrate how liberal regimes of governance emerged during the eighteenth century in response to the challenge of how to overcome the problem of war within society; how that challenge led liberal regimes to develop unprecedented techniques with which to intervene upon and control the life of societies in the production of ways of living believed to be compatible with peace. And yet how, in turn, the development of such techniques of pacification has functioned historically to exacerbate the problem of war inter-socially in ways that are especially pertinent today. In order to remove the problem of war from society, liberal regimes set about making the life of their societies into what I call *logistical life*. Logistical life is a life lived under the duress of the command to be efficient, to communicate one's purposes transparently in relation to others, to be positioned where one is required, to use time economically, to be able to move when and where one is told to, and crucially, to be able to extol these capacities as the values which one would willingly, if called upon, kill and die for.

In the context of the War on Terror the production of the logistical life of liberal societies is being pursued to new extents and with ever greater intensity. With the development of new government departments such as the Department of Homeland Security in the United States the groundwork is being laid for the implementation of new techniques of social control defined by unprecedented degrees of power over life. Understanding the risks posed for life in the War on Terror requires that we overturn the terms in which this struggle is currently represented within liberal idioms of International Relations theory. Instead of conceptualising this conflict in terms of a just war against Terror in defence and promotion of a common humanity against an enemy inimical to human life as we are currently urged to by liberal critics (Barber 2003; Elshtain 2003; Kaldor 2003), I argue, throughout this book, for a conceptualisation of it as a struggle over the political constitution of life itself; specifically over the questions of *what human life is* and *what it may yet become*. When the methods with which regimes have sought to free the life of their societies from the problem of war have demanded and achieved the incremental targeting of life itself, to the point where the most ordinary expressions of life have become objects of strategic threat, it is of paramount importance to question the idealisations of life fuelling the development of such methods. And that is precisely what each of the subsequent chapters of the book will attempt to do.

Chapter 3 develops Gilles Deleuze and Felix Guattari's account of the nomadic tendencies of life which, they argue, always undermine the attempts of any and every political regime to command and control the constitution of the life of subjects and societies. Nomadic life, in contrast with logistical life, is a life which refuses to accept and live within the boundaries determined as necessary for the production of efficiency, which seeks other principles upon which to form community with others, and which when subject to any regime which seeks to contain it spatially, discipline its use of time, or control its movements, threatens that regime with its own capacities to wage a war of movement against it. Deleuze and Guattari's theory of the relations between nomadic life, war, and modern political regimes has, like Foucault's, never been adequately addressed in the development of theories of war and peace in International Relations (Reid 2003a). In fact research in areas of International Relations informed by Deleuze and Guattari of any type is a rarity (Jabri 2005; Shapiro 2001; Lynne Doty 1999). This in spite of its centrality to their otherwise tradition-breaking and epoch-making account of the historical, social, and political development of Western civilisation to be found in the two volumes of their *Capitalism & Schizophrenia*, most especially the second volume *A Thousand Plateaus* (1999: 351–423). Throughout this latter work there occurs a powerful interlocution with Foucault's theory of the relations between war, life, and societies which has never been given significant attention, even in the secondary interpretations of their work to be found in more immediate areas of philosophy and social theory (Reid 2003a: 71–7).

Chapter 4 explores the strategies with which Terror is seeking to refuse the impositions of biopolitical order through the development of Jean Baudrillard's account of Terror as what I call *defiant life*. Defiant life is a life which, in contrast to nomadic life, refuses the powers of movement and possibility of alternative modes of communication, guarding its capacities to be obdurate, secretive and obscure. Faced with a form of power the strategy of which functions by governing life relationally, making it communicate and move efficiently, defiant life responds with a strategy of no negotiation, and with the outright refusal of insistences for communication and movement. Baudrillard's theories have received barely any serious attention in domains of International Relations in spite of the fact that much of his recent work has been concerned directly with issues of war in relation to political and social transformation. Unlike Foucault or Deleuze and Guattari, each of whom suffered it might be said, premature deaths, Baudrillard is alive and kicking, and writing on themes central to the traditional concerns of International Relations. Most recently he has written explicitly on the phenomenon of Terror and its relations to the developing global order. Similar to Deleuze and Guattari, his broader theory of modernity and the development of societies and modalities of governance developed in the form of an interlocution and antagonism with Foucault's account.

Chapter 5 examines the ways in which Terror can be understood to resist logistical architectures of governance through an account of what I define after Paul Virilio as *circulatory life*. Circulatory life is a life which in its subjection to logistical architectures of governance seeks contrary conditions for its essential mobility, fluidity and circulation. As such it pursues a counter-ideal of an alternative architecture which will provide conditions for the prosperity of circulatory life; the ideal of an architecture that lends itself to life's suppleness, allowing it to realise its essential desires for mobility, and abilities to undergo fluid alterations in structure. Virilio's work has, in spite of its unremitting focus on the role of war in the development of historical social forms, been more or less ignored by theorists of International Relations concerned with these themes. The little attention it has been given has occurred mainly in the work of James Der Derian who has ploughed a lone furrow in this regard. Yet Der Derian's work has tended to diminish the political and social dimensions of Virilio's analysis of war, reducing him to a theorist of the relationship between

war and technology for the purposes of reappraising the contemporary revolution in military affairs (Der Derian 2001; Der Derian 1998: 1–15). The
war–technology nexus is by no means an insignificant aspect of Virilio's work
and it will be revisited here, but in fact his theory of war developed in the
context of his earliest research as an urban theorist, and most especially in relation to his theory of the political and social dimensions of architectural forms.
Chapter 5 draws directly, therefore, on some of the earliest and least examined
areas of Virilio's thought to critique existing explanations for the Terror attack
of 11 September 2001 upon the architectural edifice which functioned as one of
the most flagrant representations of the liberal way of life, the World Trade
Center. And again, it does so in a way that embellishes Foucault's central claim
as to the links between organisation for war and organisation of liberal societies.

In the sixth and final chapter we turn to Michael Hardt and Antonio Negri's
account of the *biopolitical life* of what they call 'the multitude'. Biopolitical life
is a life which subverts the logistical orders imposed upon it by establishing
alternative, ever more refined systems of organisation founded upon increasingly expressive and affective methods and means of communication. Rather
than rejecting the demands for interactivity, communication, affectivity, and
meaning as was evinced in Baudrillard's account of the defiant life of Terror,
Hardt and Negri argue that life can radicalise these attributes of liberal living by
reappropriating them for other ends. In turn their work involves a shift from
understanding Terror itself to the problem of how, if at all, life can subvert its
logistical ordering without resorting to the methods of Terror as a means of
resistance. Hardt and Negri's work, most especially their second text *Empire*
(2001), is among the most well-read accounts of contemporary problems of
international relations to have been published in recent years. And yet within
the discipline of International Relations it has been received with a great deal of
circumspection (Barkawi and Laffey 2002; Shaw 2002; Walker 2002). This is not
least because Hardt and Negri choose to jettison the traditional theoretical
frameworks from within which the development of contemporary problems of
international relations are usually narrated in favour of an overtly Foucauldian
account. Their most recent text together, *Multitude*, repeats this feat in its explanation of the War on Terror as a conflict with its origins in the development of
disciplinary regimes and biopower (2004: 13). And yet theorists of International
Relations have rarely if ever sought to question or critique the veracity of the
ways in which these two pre-eminent Foucauldian thinkers actually employ
Foucault and other related thinkers to approach theoretical issues pertinent to
contemporary problems of international relations, including problems of war
and terrorism. Similar to the theorists explored in other chapters of this book
their work is defined by a search for an explanation of the ways in which life, in
spite of its subjection to logistical strategies, nevertheless escapes and resists its
subjection. Yet the means by which they theorise both the interrelation of life to

war in the context of liberal modernity, as well as the means with which they conceive the strategies of resistance which life develops to escape the confines of liberal living, are not necessarily consistent with Foucault.

In the epilogue I briefly consider where these different analyses take and leave us with respect to the War on Terror and the broader problems of relations between life, war, and politics of which this war is an expression. In the context of a war in which liberal regimes are attempting to convince their publics that it is no less than the future survival of the human species which is at stake in a conflict against an enemy stripped of all ordinary attributes of humanity, it is of necessity that we continue to question as rigorously as possible the relations between life, war, and liberal modernity. It is, as will be argued throughout, of necessity that the problem of liberal modernity no longer be understood as that of how to free life from its subjection to a historical and politically contingent condition of war, but how to free life from its subjection to the means of liberal solutions to the problem of war. There is today not so much a problem with war as such, but more pressingly with prevailing liberal solutions to war. That is to say in the limitations of the ways in which liberal regimes construe social conditions conducive to peace. Understood thus, the imperative question of politics which Foucault specified for us, which the other theorists in this book all seek to respond to, and which nevertheless continues to plague us, is that of how to disengage from the biopolitical techniques and processes through which life comes to be pacified and mobilised as logistical life. What form does life take when it is no longer suborned to a liberal teleology of peace achieved through its subjection to logistical orders? If we desire a resolution of this grand paradox of liberal modernity we must establish other ways of construing the life of human being, ones which challenge its seemingly endless polemologies and erstwhile resort to Terror. It is my hope that this book may contribute to such a challenge.

2

Logistical life: war, discipline, and the martial origins of liberal societies

THE ADVENT of the War on Terror entails implications for life within liberal societies which testify directly to the paradoxical limits of liberal modernity. In response to the emergence of Terror, we are witnessing a historic shift in the ideological underpinnings of liberal societies where the long professed belief in the possibility of a sustainable peace is being supplemented by a belief in the necessity of a perpetual war. Founded, at their inception, upon the challenge of the mastery of war in the name of a commitment to the promotion and enabling of peace, liberal societies appear today to be all but reconciled with the necessity of war as a condition for the sustenance of their mere existence. Animated by fear and insecurity at the refusal of their enemies to submit to the same processes of transformation with which they themselves have attempted to make the transition from war to peace, liberal societies find themselves today perversely haunted by the very condition which they have historically sought to escape.

Yet, as will be explained in this chapter, this paradoxical state of affairs should not be understood as a contingent failure in the development of liberal modernity. This war does not represent a momentary faltering in the otherwise progressive journey of humanity from its servitude in a condition of war to the eventual freedoms of peace. Instead, the major significance of this war is that it represents the culminating point in the development of a form of regime which has aimed, from its outset, at the subjection of the life of its societies to principles of organisation deriving directly from its own war requirements. As was argued in the introductory chapter, it is a measure of the weaknesses of theories of International Relations to date, that they have failed to rebut the ideological claims of liberalism as to its pacific project in stronger terms. Instead, theories of International Relations, even some of the more critical variants, have been complicit in perpetuating the myth that the development of the liberal way of life offers the possibility of freedom from the violence and threat of war.

In contrast, this chapter argues that what liberal regimes have achieved historically and continue to pursue today politically, is not the transformation of human life from conditions of war to peace, but the reduction of the polemical vitality of human being into what I propose to call 'logistical life'. The forms of society that liberal regimes and their proponents proclaim as peaceful are better understood as logistical orders, in which life is subjected to principles deriving from the organisational needs of those regimes for increased efficiency in preparation for war. The logistical function of the forms of life lived under liberal jurisdiction is a feature of liberal societies which few if any of the existing Foucauldian studies of biopolitical regimes of power have picked up on. In turn this chapter argues that liberal regimes have only ever achieved the forms of logistical efficiency which they have through the waging of a more or less continuous war upon the societies which they govern. The claim that the development of liberal modernity has been a process of the gradual realisation of a project of peace needs to be replaced with an understanding of liberal modernity as a process underwritten by strategies of *pacification* pursued through a range of disciplinary and biopolitical techniques deriving from the military sciences. This is the grand paradox of the liberal project first exposed by Foucault's original accounts of the function of war in organising liberal societies in *Discipline and Punish* and *The History of Sexuality*. Founded discursively as a project based upon the pursuit of peace and the enabling of humanity, the liberal project is now unravelling before our eyes, revealing its roots in an essentially logistical orientation and state of permanent mobilisation which is contrary to the integrity of life's most ordinary tendencies, and for which the military sciences have been the primary source of influence.

In the wake of the attack on the World Trade Center in September 2001, the servitude of liberal societies to the logistical needs of their regimes would appear to have become all but intractable. The President of the United States, George W. Bush, in announcing the declaration of the War on Terror, proclaimed that this war will be different to any other previous war. It will be of unprecedented length, he forecasts, and its terrains will be 'broader than the battlefields and beachheads of the past' (Bush 2001b). Two hundred and six years after the publication of Kant's definitive tract *Perpetual Peace* (1983), which laid out a plan for the resolution of the problem of war, the foremost state at the centre of the development of the liberal project, the United States, committed itself to a war with no determinable end, and of global scope; a war characterised by the likelihood of deployments of weapons of mass destruction, of biological and chemical agents, and the guarantee of further mass death. How can this paradoxical feature of liberal modernity be explained? How should we understand the relations between war, liberal regimes, and their discursive commitments to peace? How do we explain the fact that a political project predicated so fundamentally upon the ideal of peace has culminated in the exacerbation of its grand nemesis, war?

More integrally, how can we understand and make sense of the depth and complexity of the effects of this war upon the infrastructures of liberal societies currently? Exposing the weaknesses of liberal discursive commitments to peace requires not only, if importantly, that we point to the perpetuation of the violence of war internationally by liberal regimes beyond the boundaries of their own societies, in places currently such as Iraq and Afghanistan. It requires that we address the fact that the domestic realms of liberal regimes, in spite of the claims made of them as to their superiorly pacific way of life, are perversely characterised today by their involvement in the logistics of war-making. In June 2002, Bush proposed to the US Congress the creation of a new cabinet department – the Department of Homeland Security. Described as the biggest development in American federal government since the Truman administration's creation of a Department of Defense and a National Security Council in the 1940s, the Department of Homeland Security is responsible for the prosecution of the War on Terror on the home front. Addressing a threat which it itself currently describes as a 'permanent condition' (Bush 2002), effectively committing American society to a war without end, the Department mobilises United States citizens by preparing them to be, among other tasks: 'aware of your surroundings'; 'aware of conspicuous or unusual behavior'; 'not accepting packages from strangers'; not being 'afraid to move or leave if you feel uncomfortable or if something does not seem right'; 'planning how to get out of buildings, subways or congested public areas'; 'assembling a disaster supply kit at home'; and becoming 'familiar with different types of fire extinguishers' (Department of Homeland Security 2001). How is it that a form of society predicated upon the ideal of peace is today so suffused with the logic of war-preparedness? Why is it that human conduct within liberal societies is so heavily defined by logistical concerns? Why is it that the sustenance of a peaceful life within liberal societies requires such dedication to war? Why is it that the techniques that liberal societies employ to provide security from their enemies must necessarily be applied so voraciously to each and everyone within liberal societies themselves?

The purpose of this chapter is to interrogate this paradox by recovering Foucault's original account of the roles of war in the organisation of liberal societies; to demonstrate that these are not contingent features of a society meeting with a particular form of threat, nor a mere rite of passage that liberal societies must traverse in order to more fully establish an already existing condition of peace which simply requires defending and developing; and to show that the imposition of these logistical principles is a feature absolutely integral to the ways in which liberal regimes have pursued social order right from their inception. In doing so it will become possible to explain how this deeply flawed project of liberal peace came to be constructed, to trace its paradoxical logic back to the origins of its emergence, and to unearth its effects upon the societies

[*19*]

and subjects it has colonised, in the hope that we might yet establish a way of escape from it, and pursue a more meaningful and sustainable way of living out our relations with ourselves and our others.

As such we will trace the development of Foucault's articulation of the problem of war from its beginnings in *Discipline and Punish* where he locates the emergence of the military sciences, and especially eighteenth-century thought on military tactics, as among the original sources for the expression of what he termed a new form of 'disciplinary power' concerned with the transformation of the life of the human body into what I call 'logistical life'. Logistical life is a life lived under the duress of the command to be efficient, to communicate one's purposes transparently in relation to others, to be positioned where one is required, to use time economically, to be able to move when and where one is told to, and to be able to extol these capacities as the values for which one would willingly, if called upon, kill and die for. We will encounter similar and comparable formulations of the ways in which liberal regimes shape, condition and mobilise life in the work of other thinkers in subsequent chapters, but it is in Foucault's work that this formulation of the problem of life in its subjection to liberal regimes deriving their principles of organisation from war finds its foremost expression.

Moving from *Discipline and Punish* through to *The History of Sexuality*, this chapter explains how the development of Foucault's conceptualisation of the problem of war establishes the great paradox and crisis of liberal modernity. From demonstrating in *Discipline and Punish* the role of discourses and practices deriving from the military sciences in the strategies of pacification that liberal regimes pursue against their societies through the development of disciplinary power over life, Foucault shifts to focus on how the development of what he termed 'biopower' mobilises populations to wage war in the name of life necessity. In writing the first volume of *The History of Sexuality* Foucault argued that liberal regimes' subjection of life pacifies societies while exacerbating the problem of war inter-socially to the point where it is the life of the species itself that is at stake in practices of modern warfare. War figures ultimately for Foucault, in contrast with liberal and most other mainstream theories of International Relations, not as a primitive state of being against which liberal societies and their power relations can be differentiated, nor simply as realists ordinarily construe it, as a utile instrument for the pursuit of the grand strategies of states in paradoxical compromise of the civil condition of modern societies, but rather, as the integral condition of life against which politically qualified forms of life within liberal societies have been defined and mobilised to struggle. It is that integrity of life which Foucault believes, and as will be argued here, is at stake and imperilled by the application of logistical strategies aimed at securing liberal societies from the threat of Terror.

In turn, we will examine also the ways in which the responses of liberal regimes to the current threat of Terror exhibit features which, while embellishing Foucault's account of the martial origins of liberal societies, also can be argued to demand its extension and adjustment. The sociologists Mitchell Dean and Nikolas Rose, have adapted Foucault's analysis of liberal regimes to argue for a distinction between early and advanced forms of liberalism (Rose 1999a: 137–66; Dean 1999: 164–74; Rose 1993). Rose, for example, has demonstrated convincingly how practices of citizenship have changed in the development from early to advanced forms of liberalism. Advanced liberal regimes are dependent, he argues, on the activation of new powers of the citizen. 'Citizenship is no longer primarily realized in a relation with the state, or in a single "public sphere", but in a variety of private, corporate and quasi-public practices from working to shopping' (1999a: 166). Rose demonstrates empirically, by investigating a range of different social domains, how citizenship is currently performed and achieved through active participation in practices which were previously conceived in terms of services to be provided by government. Focus groups, for example, mobilise citizens to participate actively in political processes of decision-making in a shift from traditional governmental techniques of party representation. Citizens are mobilised as consumers to regulate areas of public service in displacement of the traditional roles of governmentally appointed experts. And citizens are mobilised as 'prudent' to assume responsibility for providing their own financial security in displacement of traditional roles of national schemes of compulsory social insurance.

There is, of course, a very comparable shift at work in the development of practices of war within liberal regimes. At the inception of modernity liberal regimes were able to maintain the fiction of their roles as providers of military security to societies removed from the condition of war said to define the international sphere. Today liberal regimes are able to mobilise their entire societies for the active participation in the conduct of a war which dispenses with the fiction of a boundary between national and international spheres. Rose's analysis, like almost all of the Foucault-informed scholarship within areas of sociology, neglects the role of the military dimension of society in Foucault's analysis of liberal regimes. His concept of security, indeed, is limited to a discussion of issues of economic welfare and the risk management of petty criminal behaviour (1999a: 250–63). Even in the instances where sociologists such as Rose and Dean have attempted to take on Foucault's argument with respect to the relations between war and liberal regimes, their observations have tended toward the superfluous (Rose 1999b: 15–52; Dean 1999: 139). It behoves us therefore to go where sociologists have struggled to in our mapping of the logistical imperatives underpinning the production of life in liberal societies. For if at the inception of modernity liberal regimes were concerned with the transformation of the life of human being into logistical life as a political project to be pursued and realised surreptitiously, today their interests in the promotion and defence of a form of life organised in accordance with logistical demands is all but transparent. Historically, liberal regimes argued that the mobilisation of society for war was never more than a temporary measure involving contingent incursions upon the freedom of the lives of the populations they governed. Today, in contrast, and in the context of the War on Terror, such apologies for the subjection of societies to the needs of war have been replaced by the forthright defence of logistics as a way of life. This is a feature of the relations between liberal regimes and war contemporaneously on which I will focus, and demonstrate in the final part of the chapter in examining the strategies with which liberal regimes are currently attempting to secure their 'homelands'.

Peace, discipline, and war

Throughout his later works, Foucault focuses on the ways in which liberal regimes of power emerged historically through the development of mechanisms and techniques for the shaping and conditioning of the life of their subjects and populations in contrast with the 'taking' of life and the 'letting' live that characterised more traditional regimes of power. And while this focus on the relationship between liberal regimes and life is well attested to in the secondary literatures on his work, it is still seldom acknowledged that in his concern to explore *how* liberal regimes came to develop their own peculiar techniques for the making of life, Foucault's primary focus was on their origins in the organisation for war. In this context his *Discipline and Punish* is a paradigmatic text. There, he traces the origins of those techniques to the emergence of modern military institutions and the new forms of military-scientific thought that came into being during the seventeenth and eighteenth centuries. As he describes, 'by the late eighteenth century, the soldier has become something that can be made: out of a formless clay, an inapt body, the machine required can be constructed; posture is gradually corrected; a calculated constraint runs slowly through each part of the body, mastering it, making it pliable, ready at all times, turning silently into the automatism of habit; in short, one has "got rid of the peasant" and given him "the air of the soldier"' (1991: 135). This militarisation of men, the making of soldiers, via 'the supervision of the smallest fragments' of their life and bodies, functions for Foucault as a disciplinary model that describes in essence the mechanisms of a then developing social machine to which all would become gradually subjected 'in the context of the school, the barracks, the hospital or the workshop, a laicized content, an economic or technical rationality for this mystical calculus of the infinitesimal and the infinite' (1991: 140).

Within theories of International Relations we are still taught to think about issues of military organization, strategy and tactics as discrete enterprises that concern, specifically, the interests of the sovereign power of states in extracting efficient force from bodies of men for the deployment of organised violence toward rationally grounded and objectified political ends (see, for example, Gray 1999: 17–23). Foucault's *Discipline and Punish* is important for its radically challenging account of the liberal rationalities that have actually underlain the development of modern sciences of military organisation. For Foucault the rationality of military organisation resides not only or even centrally in the violent ends toward which military force might ultimately be deployed, but more importantly in the forms of order that are mapped out in the theorisation and implementation of military organisation itself. The strategic stakes of modern military endeavours reside not simply in the clash of forces that distinguishes combat, but in the process of preparing for conflict, in the disciplining of the life of human bodies that comprise organised military forces. In a war that is being fought for political order, not among states, or on the territorial battlefields where combatants meet, but on and in the battlefield of the human body, it is the order that life assumes in and through the human body that is at stake, Foucault argued, in the struggles to discipline the body that inform the sciences of modern warfare.

In *Discipline and Punish* Foucault documents the emergence of a range of different disciplinary techniques that distinguished the new sciences of modern military organisation: enclosure, partitioning, ranking, and serialisation. These techniques, while originating within the military domain for the spatial control specifically of recruited troops, would gradually be adjusted and become applied, he argued, to societies as a whole. Sciences of military organisation provided not only the means with which to refine the control of mass armies, but a kind of model framework for a new form of thinking about social organisation that would inform the broad development of techniques by which liberal regimes learnt to govern societies.

The chapter of *Discipline and Punish* entitled 'Docile Bodies' carefully records the emergence of these techniques with attention to their specifically military remit. It was through the technique of enclosure that men came to be assembled under one roof in the form of the barracks. This technique of enclosure allowed for new forms of control and security: the prevention of theft and violence; the dissipation of fears of local populations at the incursions of marauding bands of troops; the prevention of conflict with civil authorities; the stopping of mass desertion; and the management of expenditure (1991: 142). Through the technique of partitioning, militarised groups of men were individualised. Knowing where and how to locate individuals, to control communication between individuals, to supervise the conduct not only of the mass body but the life of individualised bodies, comprised an essential technique in the development of modern military organisation. The innovation of new systems of ranking represented a further technique by which bodies were not only individualised, but cast within a network of relations of exchange, allowing for their better distribution and circulation. The organisation of serial spaces that provide fixed positions for individuals, but permitting their circulation and interchange, allowed for new forms of tactical arrangements in the composition of military forces. Foucault demonstrates with ample reference to the work of the French military tactician, Comte de Guibert, how the modern military science of tactics encapsulated this newfound understanding of the potentialities of techniques of ranking and partitioning in the production of recombinant forms of order. 'Blinded by the immensity, dazed by the multitude ... the innumerable combinations that result from the multiplicity of objects ...' Guibert mused at the end of the eighteenth century (quoted in Foucault 1991: 148).

These new disciplinary techniques in the development of the military sciences were, as Foucault shows, much concerned with the re-ordering of relations between bodies and space. Yet they were also concerned with the disciplining of relations between time and bodily activity, or what Foucault called 'the temporal elaboration of the act' (1991: 151). He documents how modern military organisation was predicated upon the development of meticulously detailed 'programmes' according to which the 'correct use of the body' would be specified in order to allow for 'a correct use of time' (1991: 152). For example, between the mid-seventeenth and mid-eighteenth centuries, ordinances developed to refine the movements across space and time of marching soldiers. While in the seventeenth century marching was only vaguely regulated to assure conformity, by the eighteenth century ordinances specified distinctions between four different sorts of marching step.

> The length of the short step will be a foot, that of the ordinary step, the double step and the marching step will be two feet, the whole measured from one heel to the next; as for the duration, that of the small step and the ordinary step will last one second, during which two double steps would be performed; the duration of the marching step will be a little longer than one second. The oblique step will take one second; it will be at most eighteen inches from one heel to the next ... The ordinary step will be executed forwards, holding the head up high and the body erect, holding oneself in balance successively on a single leg, and bringing the other forwards, the ham taut, the point of the foot a little turned outwards and low, so that one may without affectation brush the ground on which one must walk and place one's foot, in such a way that each part may come to rest there at the same time without striking the ground.
> (Quoted in Foucault 1991: 151)

As disciplinary power was concerned with the correct use of time so it was also concerned with what Foucault called 'the instrumental coding of the body' through the creation of a 'body-machine complex' (1991: 153). Foucault considered that traditional forms of subjection involved only the extraction of the product of labour, the exploitation of bodies for their surpluses. Disciplinary power, on the other hand, is about more than that. Its aim is to assure and regulate the correct procedure by which the body carries out its labour as an end in itself. In this vein, Foucault focused again on innovations that were occurring in the domain of military organization – centrally on the specifications made in the same late eighteenth-century military ordinances as to how to fire a weapon:

> Bring the weapon forward. In three stages. Raise the rifle with the right hand, bringing it close to the body so as to hold it perpendicular with the right knee, the end of the barrel at eye level, grasping it by striking it with the right hand, the arm held close to the body at waist height. At the second stage, bring the rifle in front of you with the left hand, the barrel in the middle between the two eyes, vertical, the right hand grasping it at the small of the butt, the arm outstretched, the trigger-guard resting on the first finger, the left hand at the height of the notch, the thumb lying along the barrel against the moulding. At the third stage, let go of the rifle with the left hand, which falls along the thigh, raising the rifle with the right hand, the lock outwards and opposite the chest, the right arm half flexed, the elbow close to the body, the thumb lying against the lock, resting against the first screw, the hammer resting on the first finger, the barrel perpendicular. (Quoted in Foucault 1991: 153)

All of these new innovations, reflecting what Foucault identified as a new 'positive economy' of time according to which liberal regimes of power attempted to intensify their use of time with increased speeds and increased efficiencies, resulted, he argued, from changes that were occurring in the fields of warfare and military science. The mid-eighteenth century successes of Prussia enabled by the military systems of Frederick II were the harbinger of most of these developments (1991: 154). Through the development of these techniques with which to organise for and conduct war, emerged a new object for the organisation of power relations. That new object was, as Foucault described,

> the natural body, the bearer of forces and the seat of duration; it is the body susceptible to specified operations, which have their order, their stages, their internal conditions, their constituent elements. In becoming the target for new mechanisms of power, the body is offered up to new forms of knowledge. It is the body of exercise, rather than of speculative physics; a body manipulated by authority, rather than imbued with animal spirits; a body of useful training and not of rational mechanics, but one in which, by virtue of that very fact, a number of natural requirements and functional constraints are beginning to emerge. (1991: 155)

The 'natural body' is the object of power constituted through the emergence of techniques of discipline deriving from the changing forms of warfare reflected in the developments of modern military science concerned especially with the art of military organisation. Not simply a docile body subjected in absolute terms to the manipulations of discipline, but rather a body which in being natural is defined by its own specific requirements, spontaneous needs and demands which, in turn, offer a set of constraints and resistances to disciplinary power. It is the body that disciplinary power must adjust itself to, grasp the feel of, develop intimate knowledge of, and learn to adapt from. It is the nature of a body that disciplinary power itself idealises and aims at the realisation of. This idealisation of the natural body, this recognition of the ways in which discipline aims not simply at the correction of life in the pursuit of some mechanised ideal, but rather, the pursuit of natural and organic life at the expense of a rational mechanics, becomes especially clear for Foucault in the domain of military organisation. Again he quotes from Guibert's works on tactics:

> If we studied the intention of nature and the construction of the human body, we would find the position and the bearing that nature clearly prescribes for the soldier … since the hip-bone, which the ordinance indicates as the point against which the butt end should rest, is not situated the same in all men, the rifle must be placed more to the right for some, and more to the left for others. For the same reason of inequality of structure, the trigger-guard is more or less pressed against the body, depending on whether the outer parts of a man's shoulder is more or less fleshy. (Quoted in Foucault, 1991: 155)

Disciplinary power seeks, then, to establish a subjection of the body which is first of all premised on knowing the nature of the body. It seeks to develop techniques of subjection which will allow for the recognition of the differences that pertain between individual bodies. Foucault saw these developments of disciplinary power occurring most forcefully in the field of military organisation. For example, in the gradual drawing of distinctions between periods of training and periods of practice, the separation of the instruction of military recruits from the exercise of veterans, and the creation of separate military schools for the armed services, Foucault identified the beginnings of a process of the segmentation of disciplinary time aimed at an increasing differentiation of the particular skills and requirements of individuals. This segmentation and serialisation of disciplinary activity also worked importantly, Foucault argues, to create a newly 'evolutive time' (1991: 160). Discipline subjects the individual to an evolution understood in terms of genesis. That is to say it programmes the individual to a series of graduated tasks and exercises geared toward the production of some terminal state of being. In this sense the forms of disciplinary power that Foucault saw emerging amidst the sciences of military organisation are understood as being dedicated to the promotion of the 'growth' and 'genetic development' of both communal and individual bodies. The sciences of military organisation, in their forging of the techniques of disciplinary power, were from their outset, intersecting with, and themselves contributing to, a form of thinking that was expressly concerned with understanding and asserting control over life processes.

Individuation, this essential premise of disciplinary power, owed more, according to Foucault, to developments within the sciences of military organisation and warfare than to any other domain of innovation. In drawing the frequent comparisons he does in *Discipline and Punish* between the new forms of military organisation and changes in other domains of social practice (particularly punishment, production and pedagogy), Foucault accounts for how the development of modern military sciences of organisation was enabling a new evolutionary account of the order of life. In doing so he supplements his well known account of the epistemological shift that underwrites modern social and political orders, the shift according to which human life becomes for the first time an object of knowledge and power, with reference to war. It is within the order of war, Foucault asserts in *Discipline and Punish*, that we moderns first began to fantasise of a society that would function as a machine: not a mechanical machine, but a machine that functions as a natural body; a socio-military machine 'that would cover the whole territory of the nation and in which each individual would be occupied without interruption but in a different way according to the evolutive segment, the genetic sequence in which he finds himself' (1991: 165). In constituting the natural body as the object of disciplinary power, the new sciences of military organisation also begin to conceive of populations themselves as species bodies defined by a common genesis, evolutionary patterns, and survival rates. Foucault's major assertion, attested to for the first time in *Discipline and Punish*, is that it is in war and through war that this conception of society as a living organism with all the attributes of organic life originally appeared.

Population, biopolitics, and war

Yet, from Foucault's perspective, this is only at most one half of the problem with respect to the development of liberal societies, their martial origins and propensities. Liberal regimes, while adept at pacifying populations within their own midst, have simultaneously proved very able at mobilising the same populations for the activity of war. Indeed, this is the main aim of the strategies of pacification with which liberal regimes target the polemical vitality of bodies; to render life receptive to logistical formatting while simultaneously being able to reshape life with a force that enables it to wage war in the name of life necessity. This is why, in his later text, *The History of Sexuality*, Foucault shifted his focus to address the ways in which the emergence of the liberal concern for the exertion of control over life leads to a proliferation and intensification of the problem of war between societies. As he himself observed, 'wars were never as bloody as they have been since the nineteenth century, and all things being equal, never before did regimes visit such holocausts on their own populations' (1990: 136–7).

It is in this later text, then, that Foucault outlines for us the paradox that haunts liberal modernity in ever more pressing terms. Why is it and how is it that the development of forms of society and political regimes expressly concerned with the promotion of life and the establishment of peace, has never-theless failed to solve the problem of war? Is there, he otherwise poses the question, a logic that explains the development of the liberal pacification of life and the recurring tendencies of liberal regimes to wage war in defence of the selfsame forms of life? For Foucault it is the very shift in the orientation of power to the exertion of control over life rather than the more traditional asser-tion of the right of death that explains the increasing tendencies of liberal societies toward mobilisation for war against rival subjects and populations. Under liberal conditions he argues, 'wars are no longer waged in the name of a sovereign who must be defended; they are waged on behalf of the existence of everyone; entire populations are mobilized for the purpose of wholesale slaugh-ter in the name of life necessity: massacres have become vital. It is as managers of life and survival, of bodies and the race, that so many regimes have been able to wage so many wars' (1990: 137).

Contrary to some quite influential readings of Foucault (for example Taylor 1986), he does not argue that the traditional orientation of sovereign power to the right to kill was displaced altogether by this new form of life-administering power. Rather, that a parallel shift occurs in the role of the right to kill in the operations of power to the point where it is aligned to devastating effects with the capacities of these new life-administering forces. 'The power to expose a whole population to death is the underside of the power to guarantee an indi-vidual's continued existence' he argues (1990: 137).

It is in this formula that we find Foucault making an important adjustment to and creating a new categorical distinction within the theory of disciplinary power developed in *Discipline and Punish*. The overwhelming emphasis in Foucault's theory of disciplinary power is on the implications of the entry of life into the order of power for power's control over the life of the individual body. The chapter on 'Docile Bodies' is to a great extent concerned with the new 'tactics' of power; its abilities to arrange, control and dispose of the life of the individual body. In *The History of Sexuality* we see Foucault shifting his atten-tion away from the relations between power and the individual to that of power and the population as well as from tactics to 'strategy'. No longer homogeneous in character,

> power over life evolved in two basic forms; these forms were not antithetical, however; they constituted rather two poles of development linked together by a whole intermediary cluster of relations. One of these poles – the first to be formed, it seems – centered on the body as a machine; its disciplining, the optimization of its capabilities, the extortion of its forces, the parallel increase of its usefulness and its docility, its integration into systems of efficient and economic controls, all this was ensured by the procedures of power that char-acterized the disciplines: an anatomo-politics of the human body. The second, formed somewhat later, focused on the species body, the body imbued with

the mechanics of life and serving as the basis of the biological processes: prop-agation, births and mortality, the level of health, life expectancy and longevity, with all the conditions that can cause these to vary. Their supervision was effected through an entire series of interventions and regulatory controls: a biopolitics of the population. The disciplines of the body and the regulations of the population constituted the two poles around which the organization of power over life was deployed. (1990: 139)

In developing an account of the relations between liberal regimes and the problem of war, this distinction that Foucault first draws in *The History of Sexuality* is of crucial importance. In developing power over life, a bifurcation occurs within liberal regimes with radically differing consequences for the problem of war. In their development of disciplinary techniques liberal regimes afford themselves new degrees of control over the individualised human body. That newfound docility of the individual provides liberal regimes with the ability to secure an absence of war within the civil societies they govern. Yet in their development of biopolitical techniques, focused on the collective bodies of populations, liberal regimes afford themselves a new substance for the mobili-sation of war. Given the biopolitical context in which power is now authorised,

the existence in question is no longer the juridical existence of sovereignty; at stake is the biological existence of a population. If genocide is indeed the dream of modern powers, this is not because of a recent return of the ancient right to kill; it is because power is situated and exercised at the level of life, the species, the race, and the large-scale phenomena of population. (Foucault 1990: 137)

Traditionally war functioned as a means of resolving disputes between sover-eigns whose power was based upon a basic disjuncture between themselves and their subjects. Where subjects were called upon to participate in the defence of the sovereign, such participation occurred through an exercise of the negative right of seizure by the sovereign upon the subject's body. In a biopolitical context, where power is conceived and exercised at the level of the life of popu-lations, war occurs in the form of a struggle between populations whose very existence as the expressions of the life forms they are is at stake. The participa-tion of populations in war is hence reconceived not as the product of a right of seizure, but as a positive, life affirming act. The entry of life into the order of power, while allowing for the production of a docile peace within civil societies, affords simultaneously new forms of biopolitical war in which entire popula-tions are mobilised for the defence of their way of living.

A classic example of such an inter-articulation of disciplinary power with biopower, one which Foucault focused on fleetingly, occurred in the context of Nazi Germany (Foucault 1990: 148–9). There, a regime emerged in which highly detailed systems of discipline and surveillance for the production of logistical life were coupled with a regulatory biopolitics which imbued German society with fervour for a war of annihilation against other populations. Other populations were distinguished as enemies of Nazi Germany on account of their deviation from the norms which distinguished 'people of German blood' (Dean 1999: 141–3; Peukert 1989: 208). Traditional forms of anti-Semitism did no doubt play a role in the biopolitics of Nazi Germany but the full development of Nazism involved a war declared not only against Jews, but against all those deemed 'unworthy of life'. In turn the decision as to who, by Nazism, was construed to be unworthy of life came to incorporate a wide range of subjectivities involving a broad range of techniques of discursive construction: the social failure, the misfit, the parasite, the free rider, the troublemaker, the criminal and so forth (Dean 1999: 143). Nazism was fuelled by discriminations conducted in the domain of population management organised around discourses of social utility. The idea that general distinctions could be drawn between different populations on account of their relative capacities for contribution to the logistical capabilities of society, played a powerful role in shaping the biopolitical techniques with which distinctions between worth and unworthy forms of life were made in Nazi Germany; through which perceptions of the enemies of Nazism were formed; and in formation of the values for which many Germans would in turn kill, as well as sacrifice their own life, waging war.

Nazism provided Foucault with a particularly stark example of how the development of power over life created the conditions for biopolitically sanctioned war. In the final chapter we will consider more extensively the implications of his arguments as to the relations between biopolitics and war developed further in his lecture series *Society Must Be Defended*, when we compare Foucault's account of this problem with that of Antonio Negri. Yet it would be entirely wrong to think that Nazism, or alternatively state socialism or European colonialism, are the ultimate examples of what happens to war upon the emergence of biopolitics. If we consider, for example, the means by which liberal regimes such as the United States decide which populations are 'life unworthy' and which it might therefore wage war upon, one finds similarly biopolitical techniques of construction being employed. In a recent interview, Thomas P.M. Barnett, the assistant for strategic futures at the Pentagon's newly created office for Force Transformation, describes how there exists today a global divide between a 'Functioning Core' of liberal societies and a 'Non-integrating Gap' of illiberal ones (Kennelly 2003). It is, he argues, societies disconnected from the rules and norms which define the organisation of life within the liberal core, that by dint of that failure, 'demand attention from U.S. military forces' (Kennelly 2003: 17). As Barnett argues, 'disconnectedness defines dangers. If you're looking for instability and threats to the functioning of the international system and the global economy, you're looking at this Non-integrating Gap. That's where you're going to find the transnational terrorist

networks. That's where their interior lines of communication are found'
(Kennelly 2003: 18).

The means by which the United States determines which populations fall
within the 'Non-integrating Gap', and which thus require their military attention, focus on the most banal distinguishing features. Iran, for example, is
singled out because Iranian children are not permitted to play with the popular
American children's toy, the Barbie doll. The absence of the toy from the lives
of Iranian children signals, according to Barnett, Iran's disconnection from the
'rule sets' of the liberal core and its fear of 'ideas and concepts that are challenging because they say progressive things about the role of women, individual
freedom, and the like' (Kennelly 2003: 17). The difficulties to be had in equat-
ing the Barbie doll with a progressive idea of the role of women in society escape
Barnett. But what is most important here are the biopolitical criteria which he
applies in determining which populations are enemies of the United States. The
most banal of differences between the ways of life of an Iranian child when
compared with an American one becomes the first criterion for determining the
possibility of military conflict with that society. In this sense, United States strategy relies upon a scale of calculation of enemies every bit as perverse as the racial
paranoia which informed the strategy of Nazi Germany.

If the advent of disciplinary power over life affords, then, new forms of docile
peace, it simultaneously creates the conditions for new forms of biopolitically
sanctioned war. Yet there is a further, crucial, twist to Foucault's advance of the
problem of war in relation to liberal regimes and their establishment of power
over life. In an earlier chapter of *The History of Sexuality*, the chapter entitled
'Method' we find Foucault revisiting an observation that he first made in
Discipline and Punish. At the end of the chapter on 'Docile Bodies', Foucault
made a characteristically tentative suggestion. 'It may be', he argued, 'that war
as strategy is a continuation of politics. But it must not be forgotten that "politics" has been conceived as a continuation, if not exactly and directly of war, at
least of the military model as a fundamental means of preventing civil disorder'
(1991: 168). Arguing so, Foucault insisted that the tactical models of military
organisation were of most importance for an understanding of how war invests
the order of power. The strategic discourses of states, in which war is understood as a form of activity that determines the balance of power internationally,
is of marginal importance for Foucault when considered in comparison with the
effects of the models of tactical organisation for the ordering of societies as a
whole. In his short essay, 'Governmentality', Foucault is also to be found utilis-
ing the concept of tactics to draw a distinction between regimes in which order
is attained not by imposing law on society but by seeking refined and plural
arrangements in which bodies are individuated according to their precise and
different demands and needs (2001a: 210–11). Yet in the chapter of the
Introduction to the *History of Sexuality* on 'Method' Foucault returns to this

debate, revisiting the relations between strategy, war, tactics, and power over life in terms especially relevant to our concerns. There, he reformulates the claim of *Discipline and Punish* in the style of a question:

> should we turn the expression around, then, and say that politics is war pursued by other means? If we still wish to maintain a separation between war and politics, perhaps we should postulate rather that this multiplicity of force relations can be coded – in part but never totally – either in the form of 'war', or in the form of 'politics'; this would imply two different strategies (but the one always liable to switch into the other) for integrating these unbalanced, heterogeneous, unstable, and tense force relations. (1990: 93)

In the chapter on 'Method' we discover Foucault advancing the formulation of the problem of the relations between war, power, and life in novel terms. He writes especially of the precedence of the 'strategic model' as an explanation for how and why it is 'one of the essential traits of Western societies that the force relationships which for a long time had found expression in war, in every form of warfare, gradually became invested in the order of political power' (1990: 102). But in reference to the role of a 'strategic model' Foucault is making a distinctly different argument as to the ways in which war invests political order than that of *Discipline and Punish*. In the earlier text Foucault understands war exerting an influence indirectly via the influence of tactical models of military organisation as a kind of projected social schema for the creation of a logistical order among an otherwise disordered multitude. In *The History of Sexuality*, alternatively, Foucault starts to develop an argument as to the ways in which war invests the order of political power as a kind of immanent force. The influence of war upon society does not refer simply to the discrete influence of an institutionalised military and its bodies of tactical knowledge, but to the 'multiplicity of force relations immanent in the sphere in which they operate and which constitute their own organization' (1990: 92). Here Foucault is developing a conception of war as the source of specific forms of force relations that are constitutive of power relations. War is the source that accounts for the forms of life that generate power relations rather than being the source of influence by proxy through military institutions and discourses which wield power over the life of individuated bodies.

There is, then, we might say, a relational force to the ways in which war intersects with power and life within liberal regimes as much as there is an individuating force. Whereas war is the source of the individuating techniques of discipline it is also the source of the forces that constitute power relations within liberal societies. It is the source of the forces that comprise populations biopolitically as much as it is the source for techniques of discipline that individuate bodies. It is in this context that we can understand how Foucault begins to employ the concept of strategy in *The History of Sexuality*. Disciplinary power evolves according to the development of tactical measures with which to render the life of the individuated body the object of power over life. Biopower, on the other hand, evolves through the development of strategies with which to constitute bodies in relation as populations. Tactics divide, segment, and serialise while strategies combine, integrate, and coordinate. Yet these are not antithetical features of power over life (1990: 139). There is no discontinuity, he argues, between the functioning of tactics in the individuation of bodies via discipline and the operations of strategies in the constitution of populations biopolitically. 'Rather, one must conceive of the double conditioning of a strategy by the specificity of possible tactics, and of tactics by the strategic envelope that makes them work' (1990: 100). The strategies with which the social body comes to be mobilised as a population are inconceivable in isolation from those tactical mechanisms that determine the ways in which the life of bodies comes to be individualised. This is precisely why we must collapse the traditional distinctions between logistics and strategy and speak instead of the 'logistical strategies' of liberal regimes. Affording pacificity via the development of logistical schemas that become deployed over societies as a whole, liberal regimes employ the very same principles of power over life to initiate strategies for the mass mobilisations of societies in warfare. Knowledge and control of life afford liberal peace at the same time as they afford liberal war.

Strategy in this context, for Foucault, describes the processes by which the life of individuated bodies is rendered into the logistical life of populations. In terms of explaining how it is that liberal regimes manage to overcome their commitment to the promotion of life and articulate forms of war that are waged in the name of life necessity, it is an absolutely key manoeuvre. How it is that in fixing the terms for the expression of life, liberal regimes simultaneously shape populations biopolitically, the conditions of which are established on the basis of the threats posed by life at the biopolitical constitution of societies. How it is that the aleatory tendencies of life become the enemy against which the norm of a population is defined. How it is that those norms which constitute societies, aided by the demographic sciences of population, become the foundation for wars in which the populations being defended become mobilised on their own behalf. Never was such an account of the strategies with which liberal regimes utilise their commitments to the promotion of life, and assert their right to death in the form of war, more necessary. How else might we explain the current reassertion by liberal regimes today of power over the life firstly of their own populations and secondly and more brutally over other populations in the name of a War on Terror?

And how, as pressingly, might we escape or refuse the ways in which our bodies and subjectivities are being deployed disciplinarily and biopolitically today in this war? How might we engage otherwise with the seemingly inexorable role of war in the organisation of liberal societies as well as the now seemingly 'permanent' commitment of liberal regimes globally to the waging of war? These are the questions which Foucault allows us to ask, and which will be broached throughout the rest of this book. However, before we proceed, it is necessary to bring Foucault's analysis of the problem of war in the constitution of liberal societies up to date and closer to home. To do so we must focus explicitly on the strategies currently being employed by liberal regimes to secure the logistical way of life that characterises their societies from the threat of Terror. In doing so, we can also afford an important inflection of Foucault's original theory. For, as I will demonstrate, the surreptitiousness of the project of making life logistical has all but been abandoned by the regimes of the twenty-first century which openly profess the logistical qualities and capacities of their societies. It is the capacity of life to be logistical which is now openly celebrated as the demarcation between life deemed worth defending and those forms of life deemed to threaten liberal defences. This is a shift which Foucault himself could not have foreseen but which without him we would otherwise struggle to address.

The defence of logistical life in the twenty-first century

We have seen how in *Discipline and Punish* Foucault's concern was to examine the ways in which modern sciences of military organisation emerged not simply as a resource for the waging of war by liberal regimes against other regimes, but as a technique for the pacification of their own societies through the creation of docile bodies and what I have termed logistical life. Liberal regimes have essentially, from their inception, been conducting a quiet war for the transformation of the polemical vitality of human beings within their own societies in ways that are utterly obscured from view by liberalism's own account of itself as a project of peace. In this context, the declaration of liberal regimes' war without end against Terror only serves to bring to light what was essentially true of liberal societies from their beginnings; their subjection to a form of regime dedicated not to the removal of war from social relations, but to the reduction of life to principles deriving from the organisation for war as a necessary condition of existence.

We can register the extent to which this remains the case for liberal societies in the present by looking at how liberal regimes are asserting newly voracious techniques for the pacification of the life of their populations drawn from advances in the military sciences for the mobilisation against Terror. In the wake of the 9/11 attacks, George W. Bush has provided a series of presidential directives in communication of decisions about what the homeland security policies of the United States should be. On 17 December 2003, United States' Homeland Security Presidential Directive 7 demanded the development of a comprehensive, integrated *National Infrastructure Protection Plan (NIPP)* to address the physical, cyber and human vulnerabilities of US society in the wake of 9/11. The response to the directive from the Department of Homeland Security is expressed in *The National Plan for Research and Development in Support of Critical Infrastructure Protection* published in 2004. As it describes, the task after 9/11 is one of securing the 'critical infrastructure' of US society. Critical infrastructure it defines as composed of the 'various human, cyber, and physical components that must work effectively together to sustain the reliable flow of goods, people and information vital to quality of life' in the society of the United States (NPRDSCIP 2004: 63).

In the eighteenth century, the innovation of techniques with which to increase the logistical efficiencies of armed forces was legitimised by regimes through the claim that such was necessary for the defence of the civil domain of society from external enemies. Increased military efficiency and discipline was said to be necessary and beneficial to forms of civil life, the 'quality' of which was defined by their distinction from the warlike conditions that were said to prevail beyond the boundaries of those societies. It is in critique of this type of legitimisation that Foucault's analysis, in its demonstration of the ways in which techniques for the increase of the logistical efficiency of armed forces impacted directly upon the organisation of life within the civil domain of society, is so powerful. He exposes how the methods with which liberal regimes historically prepared their armed forces for war with their external enemies provided model templates with which to subject the life of their civilian populations to unprecedented forms of control and manipulation. And how in turn liberal regimes have sought to legitimise their wars in the name of the defence and development of the very forms of logistical ways of life they were busy inculcating within and among their subjects.

Now, in the twenty-first century and in the context of the War on Terror, we are witnessing precisely the same methods of legitimisation being employed by liberal regimes, but with a radical twist. Today the argument being deployed is not, as it was in the eighteenth century, that the development of logistical strategies with which to transform the populations of the armed forces is necessary for the defence of the life of an otherwise distinctly civilian population. Today it is deemed necessary to defend the logistical life of society from enemies which threaten to undermine the logistical efficiency of society itself. In other words, in the present conditions of the War against Terror, the capacities of societies to practise a logistical way of life have become indistinguishable from conceptions of the 'quality of life' for human beings. Throughout *The National Plan for Research and Development in Support of Critical Infrastructure Protection,* one discovers the quality of life being construed in terms of the logistical capacities which in more traditional and historical terms were legitimised simply as a means for the defence of society. The docility and plasticity of human bodies, the manipulability of human dispositions, and the multifarious ways in which human behaviour can be subjected to techniques for its control and adaptation, is now conceptualised not just as a resource for the protection of liberal societies, but as that which must be defended. As the Plan states:

> Part of the challenge of infrastructure protection is how to take full advantage of human capabilities. The Social, Behavioral and Economic (SBE) Working Group in the National Science and Technology Council (NSTC) is focused on scientific research in the areas of sensory, motor, cognitive and adaptive capability of the human. Currently, the brain is unmatched by any technological system. The human brain is a semi-quantitative supercomputer that is programmable and reprogrammable by explicit training, previous experience, and on-going observations on a real-time, virtually instantaneous basis. (NPRDSCIP 2004: 63)

The quality of human life, what is understood to distinguish it from other forms of life, we are told in forthright terms, is its superior amenability to logistical transformation. Its greater capacity for adaptation and transformation is what differentiates it from other life forms. Accounts today of this form of human superiority understood in terms of amenability to logistical techniques of transformation recall in their depth and specificity the expressions of wonderment at life's malleability to be found in those military texts of the eighteenth century that Foucault's original exploration of the martial underpinnings of the disciplinary model first exposed.

> Human eyes are capable of high-resolution, stereo-optical vision with immense range, and, integrated with a highly plastic brain, make humans uniquely capable of discovery, integration, and complex pattern recognition. Human hands constitute a dexterous, sensitive biomechanical system that, integrated with the brains and eyes, are unmatched by current and near-future robotic technologies. Humans operate in groups synergistically and dynamically, adjusting perceptions, relationships and connections as needed on a real-time and virtually instantaneous basis. Human language capabilities exist and operate within a dimensional space that is far more complex and fluid than any known artificial architectures. (NPRDSCIP 2004: 63)

As Foucault's broader analysis of the development of liberal power over life documented, the emergence of the military sciences in the eighteenth century was part of, as well as constitutive of, the broader development of the life sciences. Developments in military science have always been intimately allied to developments in the life sciences more generally (Dillon and Reid 2001). In the twenty-first century context of the War on Terror we can see this alliance being cemented and further fostered in the development of new methods for the defence of liberal societies in what is known as 'human factors engineering' or HF/E. HF/E is, as the National Plan for the defence of critical infrastructure describes, 'both a science of human performance and an engineering discipline, concerned with the design of systems for both efficiency and safety' (NPRDSCIP 2004: 64). Developing since before World War II, its aim is to harness the 'cognitive, emotional and social capabilities of the human' in order to design more secure systems for the defence of the critical infrastructures of logistical life (NPRDSCIP 2004: 65); to invest in such human capabilities with a view to creating systems of infrastructure resilient to 'deceptive behaviors' (NPRDSCIP 2004: 65), 'rogue activities', and to 'insider threats' which endanger the life of individuals and populations (2004: 42).

Yet in engineering the means with which to secure the human against deceptions, rogues and insider threats aimed at it, life itself is today facing an unprecedented danger. We can ask, after Foucault, whether it is not life itself, its indeterminacy, its tendencies toward error, its creative capacities for thought and expression, which are most endangered by the unprecedented forms of controls over life being wielded and newly asserted in strategies for the securing of logistical infrastructures against Terror. 'Anyone can be' the Plan informs its readership, 'presumed to be a candidate for insider threat' (2004: 43). And indeed everyone is the candidate of this form of threat. Research and development in response to the fear of insider threats is aimed at the creation of what is called a 'National Common Operating Picture for Critical Infrastructure' or 'COP' in order to 'sense rogue behavior' not simply in pre-identified sources of threats to life but in order to be able to 'sense rogue behavior in a trusted resource or anticipate that they may be a candidate threat' (NPRDSCIP 2004: 41). As such it is deemed necessary 'that we presume any insider could conduct unauthorized or rogue activities' (2004: 42). Consequently, the movement of life, each and every possible human disposition and expression, is becoming the object of strategies construed paradoxically for the defence of the life of societies. In this context any action or thought that borders on abnormality is likely to be targeted as a potential source of threat. As the Plan clearly states, 'the same anticipation of overt damaging action by a purposeful threat can be used to anticipate an unfortunate excursion in thought or action by a well-meaning actor' (2004: 44).

In essence what is being demanded here, in the development of a 'common operating picture for critical infrastructure', is a complete mapping of the movements and dispositions of human life on a scale and with an intensity that those military texts of the eighteenth century which Foucault focused on were only able to fantasise about. The evaluation of threats for the development of a COP requires 'detailed analysis in order to detect patterns and anomalies, understanding and modeling of human behavior, and translation of these sources into threat information' (2004: 46). It requires the development of new technologies able to provide 'analysis of deceptive behaviors, cognitive capabilities, and the use of everyday heuristics' and 'the systematic analysis of what people do and where lapses do – and do not – occur' (2004: 65).

The development and application of the technologies and techniques for the analysis of 'what people do' and their 'deceptive behaviors' runs the risk not simply of endangering the aleatory condition of being human in the most general sense. It runs the risk and indeed fulfils the risk, of the violent destruction of forms of life, human populations and individuals, who through no fault of their own, are deemed to exhibit signs of anomalous and threatening behaviour. The deliberate murder of Jean Charles de Menezes, killed with five gunshots to the head fired at point blank range by British police on 22 July 2005 is a case in point. This human being described as 'unidentified male' with 'dark hair beard/stubble' was targeted on account of the fact that his 'description and demeanour ... matched the identity of a bomber suspect' (Campbell and Honigsbaum 2005). The simple fact of his leaving an apartment block thought to have been used by terrorist suspects, the simple fact that on his subsequent journey, he exited and re-entered the bus on which he travelled, and in spite of the facts that he walked, did not run, showed no sign of possessing weapons of destruction, and gave no signal of intent of any sort, he was deemed, nevertheless, to represent a divergence from a normal pattern of behaviour so serious that his life was targeted with the most deliberate violence, and he was killed. In spite of the scale and intensity with which the aim of a complete mapping of human dispositions and behaviours has been pursued, and in spite of the urgency with which today it is being implemented, the most banal and everyday expressions of life continue to fall, sometimes tragically, outside its grasp.

Life after logistics?

As it was in the eighteenth century that the fantasy of a society which functions as a type of socio-military machine, and 'that would cover the whole territory of the nation and in which each individual would be occupied without interruption but in a different way according to the evolutive segment, the genetic sequence in which he finds himself' (Foucault 1991: 165), so at the beginning of the twenty-first century, we are seeing that fantasy become reality. If we are to make sense of what it is that is at stake in the War on Terror it is going to be necessary to attempt a complete reversal of the terms in which this struggle is currently being articulated by liberal regimes of power. Rather than conceptualise this present struggle in terms of a War on Terror in the defence of a common humanity against an enemy that is inimical to life, we can better conceptualise it as a conflict over the political constitution of life itself. When the methods with which a political regime has sought to free the life of its societies from the problem of war have demanded an incremental targeting of life itself, to the point where the most ordinary expressions of life have become objects of strategic intervention, it becomes time to question its own idealisations of life.

That is precisely what the subsequent chapters of this book will do. In doing so we can advance Foucault's original account of the struggles of liberal regimes to convert the polemical life of human being into logistical life by examining the theorisations of relations between war, life and liberal regimes of power in the works of other theorists who have been significantly influenced by Foucault or have developed their own accounts of these problems in antagonism with him. In this vein we will encounter the ways in which Gilles Deleuze and Felix Guattari bid us understand the nomadic forms of life which have and still can and do resist the impositions of techniques for the transformation of life into logistical life. We will address Jean Baudrillard's theorisation of Terror itself as a form of defiant life which is explicable on account of its aversions to logistical strategies. We will, in turn, examine Paul Virilio's theory of circulatory life and consider the ways it can be employed to contextualise the 9/11 attack on the World Trade Center as constitutive of a long-running war of resistance against the imposition of logistical forms of life upon societies. And we will, in the final chapter, examine Michael Hardt and Antonio Negri's more recent theory of biopolitical life as a means with which to conceptualise the political futures of the human beyond the space and era of Terror. In each of these chapters, then, we can usefully pose the question of whether there is life after logistics, what forms such life can and possibly is taking, and whether we can envisage in these alternatives, meaningful answers to the problems of war and biopolitical regimes waging them.

3

Nomadic life: war, sovereignty, and resistance to the biopolitical imperium

IN THE previous two chapters we developed a critique of liberal claims as to the superiorly pacific ways of life established in liberal societies through their passage to and journey through modernity. In turn we developed an explanation for the ways in which liberal societies have organised and mobilised for war historically, predicated upon the ways in which they construe and have pursued peace. This account, developed through Foucault's theory of the relationships between war, modernity, and liberal societies, stands in stark contrast to the thrust of narratives developed by liberal theorists of International Relations for whom the narrative of modernity has been and continues to be an essentially peaceful one in which liberal regimes have gradually expanded their franchise to incorporate an increasing number of peoples and territories. This expansion gathered unprecedented force in the post-Cold War era when the international influences of liberal institutions, discourses, and practices increased exponentially. The development and strengthening of the United Nations, the growth and spread of liberal accounts of democracy, the proliferation of non-governmental organisations and the emergence of a 'global' civil society, the penetration of capitalism into previously non-capitalist societies, and the creation of new layers of international law, were all subsumed theoretically within the onslaught of what has come to be known both heroically and pejoratively within International Relations as globalisation. In turn, this empowerment of liberal institutions and discourses internationally served to challenge and undermine many of the most traditional assumptions made by International Relations theorists as to the defining features of international politics. At the centre of the discipline of IR, liberal theories of International Relations privileging the analysis of forms of inter-societal dependence, humanitarian intervention, and the development of global governance, overtook the traditionally state-centric approach of political realism. Leading theorists of the liberal revolution in international affairs such as Joseph Nye were quick to declare that the strategies of *realpolitik* associated with the nation-state were outmoded and 'out of sync with globalisation's promise' of new forms of transnational interdependence and liberal peace (Nye and Owens 1996).

Beyond the centre of the discipline, I and other more critical theorists of international relations have attempted to challenge such claims through the advance of a Foucauldian approach to such developments. We have argued, for example, that the increasing liberalisation of power relations internationally should be interpreted not in simplistically emancipative terms, but as the expansion of a global governmental regime concerned with the development and intensification of new forms of power over life (Dillon and Reid 2001; Duffield 2001; Dillon and Reid 2000). This latter stress on the globalisation of liberal techniques of control and domination of life is different from more conventional critiques of liberalism, such as those developed by neo-Gramscian and classical Marxist theorists of International Relations, where the focus continues to be on thematics of state power, class-based forms of inequality, and imperialism. By the end of the twentieth century, therefore, there was a dual debate in International Relations. Firstly at the centre of the discipline a debate was being had between realist and liberal accounts of International Relations. But also secondly, beyond the centre, an as important debate between Marxist, neo-Gramscian, and Foucauldian accounts. This debate was defined by a prevailing assertion within areas of thought concerned with the international that the world we were living in was being redefined by little short of a transformation in the character of power relations internationally, one which challenged traditional accounts of power across the spectrum of different theoretical approaches to the subject.

The World Trade Center attack of 11 September 2001 has been argued to challenge both liberal and Foucauldian accounts alike. With the declaration of the War on Terror by the United States, and the subsequent invasions of Afghanistan and Iraq, the global order is now widely argued to be fragmenting into a mode of organisation more anachronistic than it is novel. Faced by vital threats to their security, the major nation-states of the Western world are, it is argued, reasserting themselves territorially, militarily, and politically. Among them the United States has committed itself to a war and a strategy that has invoked descriptions and accusations of a traditional form of 'imperialism' (Eland 2002). The newfound complexities and fluidities of the global order are, it is argued, being wrought asunder by the re-imposition of a form of power and a unit of organisation enduringly modern, the sovereign and imperialistic power of the nation-state, most especially the sovereign power of the United States. The claims as to the transformational powers of liberalism and the increasingly biopolitical character of international relations that were made in the immediately post-Cold War era are exposed, it is argued, for their fragility, and ultimately their decrepitude. Consequently we are witnessing a return to a condition of international politics that some consider more consistent with models of the late nineteenth century (Cox 2003; Ali 2003).

In contrast to these assertions, the central line of argument that I want to make in this chapter is that it is a mistake to construe the War on Terror, the invasions of Afghanistan and Iraq that have followed it, and the broader reassertion of American military and strategic power globally, in the simplistic terms of the 'return' of a state-fermented form of imperialism. For sure, the 2001 attack on the World Trade Center did initiate some changes in the organisation of power internationally, but it did not forge a regression. Central to my argument is the continuing and essential role of biopolitical forms of discourse and agency in the twenty-first century. In essence, while the reassertion of the military power of this one particular state, the United States, ought to make us aware of the continuing importance of traditional forms of sovereign power, I will argue that it remains as, if not more, necessary, to concentrate on the imperial function of biopolitics here in the post-9/11 era. If we want to understand how it is that the United States is able to wage war in the terms that it is doing today, to reassert its capacities as a sovereign state, it is necessary to focus upon the roles of non-state biopolitical forms of agency in constituting and legitimising such violence. Bereft of its biopolitical context, such violence would be meaningless and impossible to sustain. In this sense it is the biopolitical which is the constitutive force within the imperial machine which we see today expanding and intensifying its controls over life globally.

Sovereignty, power, and biopolitics

Certainly it is fair to say that Foucault himself may have overstated his case as to the relative unimportance of power conceived as sovereignty, even at certain points arguing for its abandonment (2003: 42–62). And in influential interpretations of his work in recent years we have seen the concept of biopolitics being used to argue that the traditional roles of sovereign power have now been superseded by a neo-liberal order which no longer requires the state and its traditional military armouries in order to rule (Hardt and Negri 2001: 22–41). Such assertions, resting as they do upon a construal of a more or less binary conception of the relation between sovereign power and biopolitics where the retraction of one leads necessarily to the expansion of the other, should be worrying for anyone concerned with the legacies of Foucault's thought. For construing the relation so is to contradict one of his definitive theoretical ambitions, which was precisely to overcome the binary conception of relations which has so powerfully framed the major traditions of modern political and philosophical thought. In this context it is necessary that we attempt to rethink the problem of the relations between sovereign power and biopolitics in terms of their intersection and correlation as opposed to their distinction, an ambition which Foucault himself also attested to explicitly (1997b: 67).

In order to pursue this ambition we can gain greatly by bolstering Foucault's account of biopolitics and its relation to sovereign power with the theory of power developed by one of his most important contemporaries, Gilles Deleuze. Deleuze's work bears close relation to that of Foucault, and they can be said to have shared any number of theoretical and political concerns (Reid 2003a: 71–7; Marks 1998: 108–22). Indeed both developed their theories of power in a similar period of time, that of the late 1970s. Deleuze's work with Felix Guattari especially, dedicated as it is to directly rethinking the problem of the definition of sovereign power and its relations to life and war, is especially useful in this context (1999: 351–423). Tellingly, Deleuze, like Foucault, conceives the functioning of power in terms of *strategy*. This concept conveys for each of them the ways in which power's attempt to pacify life logistically is always by definition also an attempt to reconstitute and increase its war-making capacities. As was detailed in the previous chapter, we can apply the concept of 'logistical strategy' to describe the processes by which the 'logistical life' of individuated bodies is transformed by liberal regimes into the 'biopolitical life' of populations. The concept of strategy describes, then, not just those processes by which the polemical vitality of human being is transformed into logistical life, but the ways in which logistical life is conjugated to produce the biopolitical life of a social collective capable of waging war in the name of life necessity; how it is that in addressing the aleatory condition of life, liberal regimes transform that condition by shaping life logistically and biopolitically, and in doing so render life that which threatens the biopolitical constitution of the population. It is in encountering the existence of life in its indeterminacy that liberal regimes establish the conditions upon which they are able to draw the boundary between which forms of life they secure in the name of the interests of the population and which forms of life they disqualify as the source of their insecurity, and consequently, the objects of their wars. In equivalent terms, which forms are deemed constitutive of peace and deserved of life, and which forms are deemed dangerous and possible to kill.

Deleuze and Guattari identify a comparable problematic involving the relations between power, life, and war in their account of the strategy of political sovereignty. Upon their account, the sovereignty of the state form originated in its ability to territorialise nomadic warrior societies within its own constructed boundaries for the purposes of the reproduction of a sedentary society. In turn the state was able to harness the war-making capacities of nomadic societies for its own military ambitions and enterprises of urban defence and imperial expansion. Yet this colonisation of nomadic forms of life in order to defend and increase the powers of the state presiding over a sedentary community created a situation of instability and inequality within the order of sovereignty which, they argue, persists to the present. The nomadic tendency, which Deleuze and

Guattari argue can be demonstrated anthropologically and philosophically to define human life in its essence, refuses to accept and live within the territorial boundaries determined by the state. Nomadic life, in its subjection to the territorial boundaries established by sovereignty, continually threatens the sovereign with the invocation of the power of its essential tendencies for movement and war (1999: 351–423). Movement itself becomes an expression of war against the state in a context where the power of the sovereign depends upon its ability to determine and defend territorial limits. Yet this refusal of nomadic life to be bounded by the limits determined by sovereignty, its habitual recovery of its potential powers to shift and escape the boundaries set by states, and the processes of the deterritorialisation of sovereignty which this induces, becomes over time, Deleuze and Guattari argue, a constitutive function within the process of the reproduction of state power. The deterritorialising flows offset by the invocation of this war of movement against the state create new conditions upon which sovereignty is able to reassert itself, reterritorialising its boundaries anew, strategising the movement of life in redefinition of the limits of its power. It is this open and dynamic process, of wars of movement against the state, and the deterritorialising and reterritorialising processes they produce, which Deleuze and Guattari account for in terms of the strategy of sovereignty (1999: 502–3).

The similarities between these accounts of power as strategy in the work of Foucault, and Deleuze and Guattari, their shared assertion as to the complexity of relations between war, life, and power, belie some significant differences. For Foucault, as we have already seen in the previous chapter, the relation of war to power is a problem to be overcome. Liberal regimes of power effectively wage war upon life in order to shape life logistically. And they conjugate logistical life biopolitically in order that they can wage war between themselves with populations that fight in the name of life necessity. The question of how life can escape its disqualification from the biopolitical body of the population is, however, a very difficult question to answer for Foucault. The depictions of the sordid logistical life of docile bodies and the tawdry biopolitical life of populations to be found in Foucault's works would suggest that there is an alternative integrity to life different to the degraded and cheapened forms it is subject to when it enters into power relations. But Foucault's strategy of suggestion helps us little in fleshing out the actuality of its distinctions from a life subject to power; nor do they explain for us the specificities of the ways in which life comes to resist the limitations imposed upon it by liberal regimes of power. The question of why life comes to resist the logistical strategies of liberal regimes in the ways that it does, how it articulates and defines its desires and interests against those regimes in the terms that it does, is something which Foucault's discussion of life does little to resolve. In the context of the modern development of liberal societies and the various forms of resistance and struggle against power that have taken place in the period of their development, all Foucault can offer us is a general and more or less derisory observation as to their own biopolitical definition in terms of their being different assertions of 'the "right" to life, to one's body, to health, to happiness, to the satisfaction of needs, and beyond all the oppressions or "alienations", the "right" to discover what one is and all that one can be' (1990: 145).

The later volumes of *The History of Sexuality* were to some extent written by Foucault to redress these weaknesses of his work. In the second volume, *The Use of Pleasure,* he develops an account of ascesis as a means by which to conceptualise the practices by which individual subjects of biopolitical regimes of power can resist the terms of their subjection by governing themselves, inclusive of their own interpretation of their needs, interests, and desires, in generation of counter-subjective formations. Indeed, modelling his account of ascesis on classical traditions of thought, Foucault indicates that this practice can be understood as a way not simply of governing the self, but of conducting a form of combat with one's own self. As he expressed it, 'the effort that the individual was urged to bring to bear on himself, the necessary ascesis, had the form of a battle to be fought, a victory to be won in establishing a dominion of self over self (1992: 91–2). In his short essay, 'The Subject and Power', we also discover Foucault employing war and strategic discourse to tentatively explore the means by which power relations within societies might be conceptualised to allow for the possibilities of 'escape' and 'flight' (2001b: 346–8). This celebration of the possibilities of an alternative form of war or strategic relation to that which is productive merely of logistical life, one that occurs either in the space between self and self, or within the power relations that compose societies, is at odds with the broader directions of Foucault's work, and especially the critique of the role of discourses of war in perpetrating modern traditions of resistance that he developed in *Society Must Be Defended,* which we will come to in a later chapter. In any case, although offering us an outline of ways in which individual subjects can resist biopower via the model of ascesis, Foucault is reticent to endow his account with any overtly political potential, often preferring to define it in ethical as opposed to political terms (Simons 1995: 103).

In comparison, Deleuze and Guattari offer us a forthright theory of the development of liberal modernity as a political narrative in which war plays a constitutive part. Liberal modernity figures in their work as the unfolding of ever more intensive expressions of the nomadic tendency, its wars of movement against the impositions of the transcendental apparatus of state sovereignty. Upon their account, liberal modernity testifies to the one essential law to which nomadic life is capable of being faithful, that of its own immanent potentiality to be other than it is told to be by forces that exist above or beyond its own plane of existence. The nomadic tendencies of life are by definition hostile to the central principle of sovereignty, defined as it is by the ability to determine the territorial limits of what life may be and become. Yet the development of liberal regimes of power, motored by their capitalist economies, has created, Deleuze and Guattari argue, novel conditions for the elaboration of life's immanent hostility to sovereignty. As they argue, 'unlike previous social machines, the capitalist machine is incapable of providing a code that will apply to the whole of the social field ... capitalism tends toward a threshold of decoding that will destroy the socius in order to make it a body without organs and unleash the flows of desire on this body as a deterritorialized field' (2000: 33).

Deterritorialisation, this key function of the strategy of power, has never had such potential for expression as it does now in the context of the development of liberal capitalist societies. Power has never been so unlimited in its unleashing of the nomadic flows of deterritorialisation and the expression of their wars of movement against it. By this they do not mean to argue that the problem of sovereignty is upon the point of being undone by the nomadic wars of movement set in train by liberal modernity, or that the development of liberal modernity has delivered us to the precipice of a world beyond power relations. What they argue is that the capacity for the nomadic tendency of life has never been so integral to the functioning of a political and social system as it is now in the context of advanced liberal capitalist societies.

There is an abiding tendency, where the interpretation of the utility of Deleuze and Guattari's account of nomadism for International Relations is concerned, to attempt to reduce it to the phenomenon of human migration from one society to another (Lynne Doty 1999). In contrast, Deleuze and Guattari distinguish the nomad specifically from the migrant. The migrant is someone who 'leaves behind a milieu that has become amorphous or hostile', whereas 'the nomad is one who does not depart, does not want to depart' (1999: 381). Nomads are not concerned with movement from one territory to another as such. Historically nomads would resist the impositions of the ways of life of a sedentary society by holding and preserving the smoothness of the space which they occupied. Within that smooth space, not wishing to move from that space, the nomad preserves his capacity for movements denied to him under the striated conditions of sedentary societies. This is quite different from migration which is invariably from one site of striation to another in which the journey is merely an inconvenience. As such the movements of nomadic life are to be understood as intensive in distinction to the extensive mobility of migrants.

Amid liberal conditions nomadic life is expressed quite differently to the historical examples of nomadic societies that form the backdrop of Deleuze and Guattari's account of it. As Paul Patton points out, their account of nomadism is intended not simply to make a historical case but to 'controvert a deep stratum of the European social imaginary' (2000: 119). For contemporary examples of nomadism, Deleuze and Guattari's focus tends largely to be on novelists, poets, composers, playwrights, film directors, actors, philosophers, and artists who pursued experimental lines of thought or expression which escaped dominant codes in particular idioms of artistic or intellectual expression, sometimes giving birth to entirely new genres: the point being that nomadism is today, and has been for sometime, a socially disseminated practice, to be located in each and every existence in which life finds expression. There is a smack of cultural elitism to some of the examples they employ, but the ultimate nomad of contemporary liberal societies is in fact, they argue, the anonymous 'schizorevolutionary type' to be found in every social institution, in every workplace, school, barracks, factory, hospital, street, and family. The schizorevolutionary exists disseminated throughout the finer fabrics of everday life in liberal societies, contesting the transcendental constraints he encounters, inventing new ruses of escape and evasion, and in the process preserving the conditions for the inherent nomadism of life which refuses to accept and live within the boundaries determined by such societies as necessary for its static reproduction, seeking other principles upon which to form community with others, and constituting within the context of that regime the possibility of an altogether different way of life.

Yet Deleuze and Guattari's account of the contemporary expressions of nomadic life amid liberal conditions is not simply a celebration of the schizorevolutionary tendency, it is an account more acutely of how liberal capitalist societies reproduce themselves through the capture and deployment of nomadic movements which emerged at their outset as a challenge to transcendental forms of sovereignty. Liberal modernity bears witness, they argue, not simply to the gradual unfolding of improved social conditions in which nomadic life might find itself more at home, but to the perennial corruption of the nomad, his territorialisation within the machinery of social reproduction by sovereignty. The argument to be pursued in this chapter is that such a Deleuzean account of liberal modernity as an advanced expression of this struggle between forms of state sovereignty, and the nomadic tendencies of the forms of life subject to sovereignty, can be a useful framework within which to address the problem of biopolitics in this context of the War on Terror. The current reassertion of the sovereign power of the United States amid the War on Terror is itself only explicable, I argue, in the context of a reterritorialisation of biopolitical discourses, practices and institutions which emerged at their origin as challenges to the territoriality of the nation-state form. The deterritorialisations of state sovereignty affected by the development of biopolitical bodies over time have created the precise conditions in which the sovereign power of the United States is today being reasserted with such reterritorialising effect. For this reason we can see that accounts of international relations after 9/11 which insist upon reading contemporary US strategy as a reassertion of a traditional form of sovereignty that compromises the complex systems of global liberal governance created during the 1990s, are overstated in that they neglect the integral logistical roles that biopolitical forces continue to play in the strategy of power internationally today. In being so, such accounts place too great an emphasis on the role and agency of the government of the state, and especially the discursive shift that has occurred within United States foreign policy and in the articulation of its strategy since the declaration of the War on Terror. A closer analysis of the ways in which the War on Terror is being conducted, with particular focus on the War on Iraq, can demonstrate the continuing importance of biopolitical forces in the constitution of power internationally today.

If it is important to account for this reassertion of sovereign power in relation to biopolitical forms of agency and practice which by definition compromise the sovereignty of the nation-state, it is as important to address the question of how we might go about deterritorialising the imperial function of these agencies and discourses. As such I want to think about what the consequences of such a Deleuzean reading of the strategy of sovereignty are for prevailing understandings of the potential for our ability to respond to and resist the War on Terror today. Interpreting the War on Terror, International Relations theorists are still largely trapped within the narrow confines of debate between realist and liberal positions (Kagan 2002: 113). Can the codification of international law and the development of liberal international institutions posit a solution to the problem of sovereignty? Or does sovereignty always, by necessity, override the potentials for a cosmopolitan world order? These are the kinds of parameters that, in the face of the complex changes presaged by the War on Terror, we still see being used to frame debate within International Relations theory in the twenty-first century. Attempting to think problems of the relations between law and force in such dichotomous terms forges the kinds of simplistic characterisations of international order in terms of anarchy *or* order that sustains the age-old dialectic of realism and liberalism, which remains a powerful motor of International Relations theory (Hutchings 1999: 1–54). One of the many differences that the Deleuzean analysis advanced in this chapter can make is to help us think more directly about the importance of the *collusions* between sovereign and biopolitical forms in the development of global liberal regimes today. The development of international organisations, of international law, the codification of human rights, the range of liberal aggressions at work in the onslaught of globalisation, are all features of a set of forces that can only superficially be distinguished from the modern institutions of sovereign state power. There is continuity between the form of sovereignty with which nation-states still today utilise force in breach *of* law and the sovereignty with which the most narrowly biopolitical account of man is enforced *through* law by humanitarian and other liberal actors in the world today. This is something which International Relations theory still struggles to recognise. If we want to resist the reassertion of the form of sovereignty at work today in the context of the War on Terror it is essential that we expose this complicity of law and force: in other terms the complicity of the biopolitical and the sovereign, and attempt to deter-ritorialise the conditions upon which the limits of this debate have been constructed.

The rest of this chapter will proceed thus. In the following section I will give a brief account of how the War on Terror is being interpreted through the trope of sovereignty. I critique such accounts for their overemphasis upon the role of the shift in the discourse of government and foreign policy in the US as an explanation for the war as an unbridled reassertion of sovereign power. In the third and fourth sections I demonstrate the extent to which the actual deploy-ment of US sovereign power in the context of the War on Terror remains conditioned by features that are continuous with the new forms of biopolitical agency and discourse which emerged in the 1990s. And in the fifth and final section I reflect on where this analysis takes and leaves us in terms of our abili-ties to resist the imposition of this war. In attempting to do so it is imperative that we address not simply the problem of sovereignty as it is narrowly conceived within international relations, but focus on the violent legacies of the liberal humanist politics which have empowered the development of biopoliti-cal forms of agency which at their outset were conceived as a challenge to sovereignty. More so is it necessary that we avert the fall into the cheap human-ist traps currently being set by thinkers concerned with the promotion of a global liberal civil society as a response to the phenomenon of Terror. Moreover we must repose the question of what life is and may yet become outside of or beyond its logistical and biopolitical parameters. In a basic sense this is to pursue the possibility of a Deleuzean resolution of the question which Foucault's own theorisation never quite succeeded in answering. Is it possible to pursue a politics that deterritorialises the sovereign power of the state without being reterritorialised by it? Can we deterritorialise life from its subjection to the logistical demands of modern forms of sovereignty without life itself succumb-ing to the function of a biopolitical imperium? To pose the problem in these Deleuzean terms is a useful exercise in so far as it allows us to retheorise the rela-tions of life to power and war in ways that are possibly more productive and future oriented than Foucault's own theory might allow for.

The 'return' of imperialism?

Those who assert that we have witnessed a regression in the organisation of power internationally since 9/11 point to the contingencies of the global politi-cal order during the 1990s (Cox 2003: 13–14). The end of the Cold War, it is said, bequeathed the United States a preponderance of power internationally. The absence of a symmetrical threat to that preponderance allowed the US, under the auspices of the Clinton administration, to embark upon a liberal internationalist strategy that involved the cultivation of new forms of interdependence and connectivity. The shift in administrative power nationally within the US coupled with the World Trade Center attack provided the grounds, it is now argued, for a change of direction in US foreign policy and the consequent return to a more traditionally unipolar and ultimately, imperialist world order (Dunn 2003). As Michael Cox describes, the intellectual groundwork for a reassertion of US imperialism had been carried out some years in advance of the 9/11 attack. As early as 1997, the American neo-conservative think tank, 'Project for the New American Century', dedicated to the reframing of the Republican agenda, was arguing for the 'restoration of a foreign policy of American leadership' based on 'the three M's of American foreign policy ... Military strength, Morality, and Mastery'. Not only was it the case that the increasingly liberal organisation of international politics during the 1990s was perceived to threaten the 'national interest' of the US, but there was also a sense in which a more fundamentally normative commitment to the defence of the international state system was at stake. The War on Terror itself has been conceived within the US in terms of an attempt to defend the very form of the nation-state and the international state system from the incursions of a threat shaped and conditioned by the impact of liberal internationalism. 'International terrorism is not dangerous because it can defeat us in a war, but because it can potentially destroy the domestic contract of the state by further undermining its ability to protect its citizens from attack' wrote Audrey Kurth Cronin after the 9/11 attacks (Cronin 2002). The form of threat posed by Terror appears to have been interpreted by the Republican right within the US as that of an advanced expression of the deterritorialising flows set in train through globalisation. The War on Terror has been articulated within areas of the US foreign-policy establishment as a commitment to a defence of the traditional values and sovereignty of the nation-state against that deterritorialising threat. The current strategy of the US is articulated in these terms as an attempt to force a regression within the international system to an older, more reliable form of order; a regression that secures and re-enforces sovereign boundaries against the encroachments and malign insecurities forged through the development of more overtly liberal power relations.

One of the most appealing ways to account for twenty-first century US strategy as initiating a return to imperialism is to consider the copious amounts of imperialist rhetoric surrounding the current Bush administration. One of the most remarkable features of the current articulation of US foreign policy is an apparently naked commitment to imperialism. The US has throughout much of its history been accused of pursuing an imperialist agenda. Customarily, however, the foreign policies of the US have been accompanied by discursive commitments to democratically anti-imperialist ends. The current reassertion of American power is, it would appear, avowedly imperialist. 'Mastery' is a positive term of reference within the lexicon of American foreign policy of the twenty-first century and its concomitant condition of possibility – 'enslave-ment' – an inferred aim of American strategy. Traditionally, international relations theorists are used to dealing with orthodoxies that either discount the role of structural economic and political inequalities within the international system as unimportant for our understanding of how that system functions (realism) or which account for those inequalities as contingencies that the system itself is in the process of overcoming through the development of democratisation (liberal internationalism). In turn we are traditionally accus-tomed to critiques of those orthodoxies which demonstrate how essential the production of inequality and unevenness is to the existence of the international system (Marxism). At the turn of the twenty-first century the reversal in the order of these debates may from some perspectives have appeared puzzling. Neo-conservative discourses on the international system appeared to be naked in their ambitions for the possibility and pursuit of a state-centred form of imperialism while critical accounts of International Relations were increasingly insisting on the decrepitude of the political form of the nation-state amid the increasing liberalisation of International Relations occurring in the post-Cold War era.

The current state of world politics has made, from the perspective of many, Foucauldian claims as to the prevalence of biopolitical forms of power over sovereign state power in international politics look naïve. Critical appraisals of the War on Terror continually make reference to the discourse of the neo-conservative wing as if it were an unproblematically descriptive account of the deployment of US power (Ali 2003; Cox 2003: 13–14; Bleier 2002: 35–42; Eland 2002: 5). Yet such critiques of the War on Terror that buy into the regime's own account of it as a return of imperialism ignore the vital roles played in its conduct by agencies, practices, and discourses of biopolitical form. The discur-sive attempts among the Republican right to qualify American foreign policy today in terms of imperialism are, in a certain sense, curiously out of sync with the actual deployment of the sovereign power of the US internationally. The assertion of the sovereign power of the United States occurring during the War on Terror remains conditioned by the continuing roles of agencies and practices that emerged in the 1990s, empowered by the deterritorialisation of the sover-eignty of nation-states and the advance of liberal institutions and actors. Here I am thinking chiefly of the roles of the United Nations and the range of non-governmental actors who defined the shifts in power that occurred in the post-Cold War period. These agencies and their practices remain crucial both to the logistical efficacy as well as assertions of legitimacy accompanying the reassertion of US sovereign power. It is fair to say that the emphasis on the prevalence of biopolitical forms and forces at the expense of the traditional units of sovereign power should not be overstated. Nevertheless, in order to compre-hend the strategy at work in the organisation of power internationally today we have to examine the intersections of sovereign power with these new forms of biopolitical power which arose nominally in deterritorialisation of the state. It is of great importance indeed that we pay heed to the role of these agencies and their practices. This chapter redresses this imbalance.

Rethinking sovereignty in the context of the War on Terror

To better understand the ways in which biopolitical and sovereign forms of power are intersecting in the context of the War on Terror we can develop Deleuze and Guattari's theorisation of the strategy of sovereignty which they detail in their two volume work, *Capitalism and Schizophrenia*. In the first volume, *Anti-Oedipus*, Deleuze and Guattari apply their theory to the international system directly. The international system, they argue, oscillates continually between two opposing tendencies that are inextricably bound up with one another: the schizoid revolutionary tendency and the paranoiac fascistic tendency. As they describe,

> The social axiomatic of modern societies is caught between two poles, and is constantly oscillating from one pole to the other. Born of decoding and deterritorialization, on the ruins of the despotic machine, these societies are caught between the Urstaat that they would like to resuscitate as an overcoding and reterritorializing unity, and the unfettered flows that carry them toward an absolute threshold. They recode with all their might, with world-wide dictatorship, local dictators, and an all-powerful police, while decoding – or allowing the decoding of – the fluent quantities of their capital and their populations. They are torn in two directions: archaism and futurism, neoarchaism and ex-futurism, paranoia and schizophrenia. They vacillate between two poles: the paranoiac despotic sign, the sign-signifier of the despot that they try to revive as a unit of code; and the sign-figure of the schizo as a unit of decoded flux, a schiz, a point-sign or flow-break. They try to hold on to the one, but they pour or flow out through the other. They are continually behind or ahead of themselves. (2000: 260)

Deleuze and Guattari's theorisation of the necessary intertwinement of processes of deterritorialisation with those of reterritorialisation provides us with a more helpful framework for comprehending the apparent reassertion of the sovereign power of the United States in the context of what appeared in the 1990s to be an ever-increasingly deterritorialised global order. There is no necessary dynamic within the development of liberal modernity toward some kind of final deterritorialised condition at the expense of state sovereignty. Rather we can understand the contemporary moment in the development of the organisation of power internationally as the articulation of this basic oscillation in the balance between deterritorialising and reterritorialising forces. This act of reterritorialisation, that by which the state reinstates its sovereignty, redrawing its boundaries in constitution of a milieu of interiority, necessarily draws upon and requires the existence of deterritorialising flows. Indeed we can only understand the global scope with which the reterritorialising force of sovereign power is being asserted today in the context of the global flows through which the deterritorialisation of the power of nation-states was rendered during the 1990s. The global assertion of state sovereign power that is occurring in the context of the War on Terror assumes as its condition of possibility the existence of spaces, practices, and discourses created by the very bodies that deterritorialised sovereignty during the 1990s. This is an integral element of the War on Terror that is ignored in those accounts of it as a return of a traditional form of imperialism. In spite of the discursive commitments to an imperialism that revokes reliance on allies, champions the national interest, neglects the importance of norms, and that eschews moral and ethical underpinnings, the War on Terror is conditioned by flows, agencies and practices of biopolitical form.

We can start to think about this problem concretely in the context of the War on Iraq. One of the major features of the immediately post-Cold War era was the expansion in the aims and ambitions of the United Nations. There was a new optimism as to the potential of the United Nations to fulfil the humanitarian tasks of its Charter (Messner and Nuscheler 2002: 125–55). There was a widespread belief that the burgeoning strength and scope of the United Nations represented a shift away from an international system predicated on the sovereignty of nation-states to a supranational and decentred global system that would enfranchise the deterritorialised life of humanity against the sovereign power of nation-states. The most immediate and major initiative of the United Nations at the end of the Cold War was the imposition of a comprehensive sanctions regime upon the state of Iraq on humanitarian grounds (Alnasrawi 2001). The Iraqi state was targeted by the United Nations on account of what is described in Resolution 688 as 'the repression of the Iraqi civilian population in many parts of Iraq', most especially Kurdish peoples (Malanczuk 1991). Perversely, the sustaining of the sanctions regime throughout the 1990s itself created a more general humanitarian crisis throughout the Iraqi population. This led ultimately to the creation of the oil-for-food programme that mediated the sale of Iraqi oil in return for economic assistance to Iraq up until the war in 2003. The oil-for-food programme developed from the provision of economic help and basic humanitarian assistance to the involvement of the United Nations in the wholesale redevelopment of the infrastructure of the Iraqi state. From its inception in 1995 it expanded gradually beyond an initial emphasis on aiding the provision of food and medicine to incorporate, by 2002, infrastructure redevelopment in a vast range of different sectors: food, food-handling, health, nutrition, electricity, agriculture and irrigation, education, transport and telecommunications, water and sanitation, housing, settlement rehabilitation, demining, assistance for vulnerable groups, oil industry spare parts and equipment, construction, industry, labour and social affairs, youth and sports, information, culture, religious affairs, justice, finance, and banking (United Nations 2005a). The programme was regarded as effective in so far as it disciplined the Iraqi state to dedicate funds deriving from the sale of oil to its population rather than to military investment (Yaphe 2003). In important senses it appeared to represent a biopolitically defined programme in so far as it aimed at an increase of the welfare of the Iraqi people at the expense of the sovereign will of the Iraqi state.

The US-led War on Iraq was widely held to represent a direct challenge to the agency, practice, and normative framework underlying UN involvement in Iraq. The humanitarian elements of UN policy, always hotly contested, were swept away, it was said, by the flagrant pursuit of US security and economic interests. Consequently we witnessed in the run-up to the conduct of the War on Iraq a new and significant split between the United States and the United Nations as well as the broader community of NGOs dedicated to biopolitical ends (Ikenberry 2002: 81). Yet the development of the UN oil-for-food programme ultimately served a central role in the organisation of the War on Iraq. The conduct of the War on Iraq by the US was predicated logistically on the existence of the dense infrastructures created by the UN in Iraq through the oil-for-food programme for humanitarian ends (MacGinty 2003: 606). The adoption of resolution 1483 led to the official establishment of relations between the UN and the occupying forces in Iraq and the transferral of responsibilities of oil-for-food activities to the provisional authorities representing the occupying powers (United Nations 2005b). Indeed, the broader framework of the War on Iraq conducted by the US was fairly consistent with the development of so-called 'liberal' or 'humanitarian' warfare during the 1990s in which the UN often played a fore-frontal role. The Bush administration went to inordinate lengths to secure the support of a range of different non-governmental and humanitarian actors in advance of the actual conduct of the War on Iraq. Having established an inter-agency group for the planning of post-war relief and reconstruction in Iraq, it then held multilateral and bilateral meetings with NGOs in order to pre-plan the reconstruction effort. Financial aid was provided to enable the United Nations High Commissioner for Refugees and humanitarian agencies to pre-position humanitarian aid. Warehouse spaces were paid for in neighbouring Gulf states in which to store humanitarian supplies (MacGinty 2003: 606). The practices of social reconstruction were integrated as fully as possible within the military operation of intervention in ways continuous with guidelines as to 'best-practice' developed in recent years by the UN itself (MacGinty 2003: 607). The War on Iraq was, in important senses, a conflict fought along biopolitical lines.

In this sense we can see that the conduct of the War on Iraq was not defined in simple terms by the naked expression of the sovereign power of the United

States that has been attributed to it in critical responses. The verbalisation of disputes between the US and the international community draws a thin veil over a thick set of logistical relations that continues to combine the sovereign power of the US with a range of biopolitical bodies and forces. In spite of the ways in which the US' use of force circumvents traditional United Nations norms, in logistical terms relations between the US, the UN and the broader realm of global civil society remain very strong. Contrary to popular perceptions of a US that is 'operating in the world on its own terms' (Ikenberry 2002), US strategy remains predicated in important respects on the securing of logistical support from a range of biopolitical bodies and agencies among which the UN is central. The claims that in pursuing a 'neo-imperial agenda' the was neglecting the need to build coalitions of states and multilateral agencies to orchestrate aid and assist in rebuilding states are wide of the mark (Ikenberry 2002). The invasion that took Iraq by storm in the spring of 2003 was a complex amalgam of forces combining the sovereign power of the United States with the biopower of a range of deterritorialised actors.

The support of forces of deterritorialisation for the War on Terror is not merely logistical. Their logistical support is born from a shared normative commitment to the conduct of the war too. Throughout the 1990s, thinkers at the forefront of liberal political thought, humanitarians, as well as various non-governmental organisations concerned with pursuing a humanitarian agenda, lobbied for a more forceful approach to human rights abuses in states such as Iraq and Afghanistan. Leading humanitarian thinkers and commentators such as Michael Ignatieff bemoaned the 'extraordinary gap between rhetoric and performance' within the human rights policies of Western powers (2001: 209). Humanitarians may object to what they perceive to be strategic limitations that nation-states impose upon the forms of militarised interventions they pursue in the name of human rights. This was a continual feature of the liberal critique of the character of the development of humanitarian war during the 1990s (Kaldor 2003: 133–4). They may also object to the failures of nation-states to pursue humanitarian causes in cases of conflicts that emerge outside the realm of their material self-interests (Ignatieff 2001: 201). Yet, ultimately, when liberal humanitarians target specific nation-states for their chastisement, such as Iraq and Afghanistan, when they demand a more forceful approach to the problems of human rights abuses, they create the discursive conditions for the reassertions of sovereign power that we have witnessed in the cases of the US-led Wars on Afghanistan and Iraq.

So many of the current critical appraisals of the War on Iraq point to its supposedly 'unilateral' character. Yet in doing so they ignore the vital roles that humanitarian-based forms of argument played in legitimising the war and most especially the continual citation of UN resolutions in support of the war. In waging war on Iraq the American and British governments were able to make recourse to the perceived failures of Iraq to implement specific UN security council resolutions 678, 687, and 1441 (Roberts 2003). No matter that there may have been no direct authorisation from the UN for the use of war against Iraq. The United States was able to draw on an indirect or implied form of authority through its interpretation of edicts directed at Iraq by the United Nations throughout the 1990s.

The strategy of sovereignty in the twenty-first century

What does this tell us, then, about the organisation of power internationally amid the War on Terror? Does the War on Terror represent an increasingly unilateral expression of the sovereign power of the United States? How can we understand the ways in which the sovereign power of the nation-state relates to the prevailing powers of biopolitical bodies such as the United Nations, the NGO community, and the broader bases of global civil society in this context? Are those latter powers, so definitive of the developments of the 1990s, now simply on the wane? Are we witnessing as a result of the War on Terror the abuse and subordination of biopolitical agencies and discourses to the self-interested strategies of state sovereignty? How can we theorise the interrelation and co-development of sovereign and biopower in the conditions of the twenty-first century?

Currently within International Relations theory we see this debate being articulated in terms of competing conceptions of the possibilities for a biopolitical global order in which a universalised humanity is enfranchised against the sovereign power of nation-states. The reassertion of the sovereign power of particular Western states amid the War on Terror is being variously interpreted as (a) an attempt to defend an already existing, biopolitically grounded system, in circumstances of an exception that demands a suspension of the biopolitical principles that define the system itself or (b) confirmation that commitments to the development of a global biopolitics that challenges state sovereignty are doomed to fail. Either sovereignty is seen to be tragically suborning the biopolitical or the sovereign is seen to be enacting a temporary and contingent transgression of the development of biopolitics in circumstantial defence of it. Both standpoints rest on an assumption as to an inherent distinction between the sovereign and the biopolitical which contrasts with the Deleuzean position we are building here where the relationship between the two is understood in terms of their necessary and functional intersection. Foucault's own thought, while testifying to such an ambition, struggled to bring to fruition the precise nature of that intersection and function. It is in this context that we can more usefully turn to Deleuze and Guattari's theorisation of sovereignty as strategy in order to provide a more critical explanation of the contemporary form of the relation between the sovereign and the biopolitical.

To do so we can start by drawing a distinction between what Deleuze and Guattari account for as processes of deterritorialisation and reterritorialisation on the one hand, and the relation of sovereign power to biopolitics on the other. We can argue, after Deleuze and Guattari, that it is only through a consequent process of reterritorialisation that forces of deterritorialisation are rendered biopolitical. The constitution of biopolitics is a tactical effect of the strategy of sovereignty. Its efforts at reterritorialisation are revealed in the biopolitical forms by which deterritorialising forces are brought back within the realm of sovereign control. The biopolitical is never a naïve representation of a deterritorialising movement outside of and beyond the state, but is defined essentially by the imprint of a reterritorialising manoeuvre. In this sense, the distinction between the immanent and nomadic movements of deterritorialisation in contrast with the sovereign's attempts at reterritorialisation can never be understood in terms of simple opposition. The movement of nomadic life toward its deterritorialisation from power always functions within a Deleuzean framework not of simple opposition to the transcendental form of political sovereignty, but in reconstitution of it. The nomad is haunted by the forms of transcendence that it attempts to ward off (Kistner 2004: 250). Each nomadic movement in aversion of sovereignty resituates life in relation with new horizons transcendent of it, giving form to a particular mode of being. No war, of whatever intensity of becoming, can release life from its situation in relation to transcendental forces of one sort or another. Life, instead, must continually reproblematise its capacities to realise its potentialities in aversion of those forces which appear upon its horizon, constituting transcendental relations with it.

This problem will be returned to in the sixth chapter when we encounter Antonio Negri's attempts to conceptualise a war which destroys life's relations to the transcendental and establish a purely immanent mode of being. Negri, as we will see, develops the concept of biopolitical life in an affirmative dimension. In the Deleuzean framework we are building here, however, biopolitical life figures as the form that a nomadic life assumes under conditions of its subjection to new lines of transcendence. When we speak of biopolitics, therefore, we are speaking of political agencies and practices that reconstitute the problem of political sovereignty. The key institutions and actors of the liberal international order today, that is the United Nations, the NGO community, and global civil society, are to be understood in this context: that is as agencies that do not simply enact a deterritorialisation of sovereignty, but rather which configure the reterritorialisation of deterritorialising flows in the reconstitution of sovereign power. Yet in this context it remains essential to pose the question of how these tactical relations between nomadic life, biopolitics and sovereignty are affected. What is it that is being deterritorialised and how is the reterritorialisation of these agencies enabled?

The defining feature of the development of modern international relations has been the ongoing conflict between the sovereign powers of nation-states that emerged at the onset of modernity and the development of liberal humanist discourses and practices generated in pursuit of an ethical commitment to the enfranchisement of a universalised humanity. Yet the account of humanity rendered in the institutionalisation of biopolitical practices and through the creation of agencies for the defence of the rights of humanity in universal terms, is itself a statically imperial one. Defining humanity in accordance with internationalised laws, reducing it to another imperial injunction, biopolitical modernity plays into the hands of modern sovereignty. Coordinating its global deterritorialisations of biopolitical life via a concomitant universalisation realises the conditions for the imposition of new forms of transcendental sovereign power, also, on a global scale. Global deterritorialisations beget global reterritorialisations. The idea and pursuit of a universally coded and legally enfranchised humanity invokes necessarily the idea and pursuit of a universal state. It is for these reasons that we cannot account for the globality with which the sovereign power of the United States is asserted today other than in the context of a global biopolitics.

Contesting sovereign power

What then are the implications of this argument as to the strategic intimacy of relations between sovereignty and biopolitics for political engagement with the reconstitution of international relations in the twenty-first century? In what ways does underlining the liberal underpinnings of the organisation of power today help us think about engaging with and resisting it? It suggests that not only ought we to be sceptical as to the capacities of liberal agencies to impose normative restraints on the exercise of sovereignty, but that we need to think more closely about how the articulation of the problems of *what human life is* and *what human life may yet become* among modern biopolitical agencies constitutes itself a form of sovereignty that is every bit as imperial as the kinds of transcendental religious forms of authority which the humanist tradition originally defined itself against. In the midst of a conflict where we have seen the headquarters of the International Committee of the Red Cross deliberately targeted it is time to recognise the limits of a humanism that imposes itself with all the vigour of such religious creeds. Some have argued that such recognition does not have to lead to the rejection of humanism as such. Instead it can be read as a demand for a return to the question of how to enact a humanist politics that does not fall party to the universalisation of its values, or attempts to secure them within institutionalised or procedural frameworks, such as those created within the biopolitical context of the contemporary international order (Gilroy 2004: 13–21). In many senses such demands resonate with the more expressly Deleuzean question of whether is it possible to pursue a politics that deterritorialises the sovereign power of the state without being reterritorialised by it. Can we deterritorialise human life from the various and arbitrary forms of authority that it is subject to without humanity itself being rendered biopolitical?

It is doubtful, however, whether this problematic Deleuze poses for us can be sufficiently responded to through the resources of the humanist tradition which thinkers such as Paul Gilroy, and before him Frantz Fanon, have attempted to invigorate (Fanon 1986). When humanism is called to respond to these basic questions, the questions of what life is and what life may become, its imagination is curtailed by the fear of life's immanent, nomadic unpredictability. The question of diversity, of the different forms which life may assume, irrespective of its nomadic potentiality and desire for difference in and of itself, has always tended to be suborned to the imperative of the defence of forms of life that already exist. 'Let us educate our children to give answers ranging from +1 to −1 on a seven point scale; that will ensure the tolerance of variability which alone can incorporate our innate diversity' argued H.J. Eysenck in his classic 'Humanism and the Future' (Eysenck 1968: 270–1). The security of biopolitical life requires the command of the logistical infrastructures through which biopolitical life organises itself. In the process the very essence of life, its innate indeterminacy and nomadic capacity for movement and variation, is withdrawn from it in the interests of the defence of the norm. Hence the humanist desire to secure the conditions of humanity becomes itself a declaration of war upon life in its aleatory condition, a form of biopolitical war waged upon the possibility of difference in and of itself; a war based around the demarcation of difference between those forms of life which constitute the conditions for the survival of biopolitical life and forms, the existence of which do not contribute to those conditions, and subsequently may die or be killed.

In their final major work together, *What is Philosophy?*, Deleuze and Guattari recognise this problematic directly. 'Human rights say nothing about the immanent modes of existence of people provided by rights' (Deleuze and Guattari 1996: 107). In this context where the idea of the human is used as a destructive imposition and a ground for violent intervention upon the processes by which the immanent, nomadic potentiality of life itself is expressed we must, Deleuze and Guattari argue, feel only 'the shame of being human', and experience the 'ignominy of the possibilities of life that we are offered' within the narrow confines of what we are allowed to be and become biopolitically (1996: 107). Better to die an animal, they argue, than to live the ignominy of the liberally enfranchised life of biopolitical human being.

To invert the biopolitical distinction between the human and the animal in these Deleuzean terms is pressing in so far as it is offers us the glimmer of the possibility of a different response to the security problematics posed by the War on Terror – a response different in measure to the increasingly aggressive responses to it from the liberal theorists of International Relations who continue to push their project of a 'global civil society' as if it were a feasible alternative by which to salvage modern liberal and humanist ideas from the wreckages of their hostilities. In the wake of the 9/11 attack upon the World Trade Center, Mary Kaldor, one of the key exponents of the idea of a global civil society, called for the further extension and strengthening of international humanitarian law (Kaldor 2003: 156). The global civil society is pitched, according to Kaldor, in a direct struggle with both the Bush administration and Al Qaeda to 'bring the "inside" of human rights and democracy home' (2003: 159). Douglas Kellner, another advocate of the global civil society approach, calls for the establishment of a 'global campaign against terrorism' and a reorientation of the agenda of the 'anti-capitalist globalization movement' to fight terrorism, militarism and war (2002: 158). Benjamin Barber argues that the creation of 'a just and inclusive world in which all citizens are stake-holders is the first objective of a rational strategy against terrorism' (2003: 88). Incredibly, in the context of a war in which liberal regimes find themselves pitched against an enemy whose hostility is articulated in the terms of an attempt to retrieve the integrity of the possibility of *another* response to these problems of the ontology of life, liberal dissidence expresses its yearning for a yet more incessant pursuit of its humanist ideals. In the midst of the rejection of the sovereign imposition of liberal humanism, dissident voices within liberal societies call forth the greater extension of the central principles of the selfsame humanist project. In the midst of the rejection of law the demand is to pursue the law more rigorously. The actions of the enemy are deemed 'predominantly the consequence of pathology and yield neither to rational analysis nor understanding' (Barber 2003: 76), and 'dialogue' it is said 'is not possible with such groups' (Kellner 2002: 158).

In historical context it is necessary to recognise the importance of the humanist attempt to enfranchise humanity in excess of the territorial sovereignty of nation-states. Yet here, at the turn of the twenty-first century, we are witnessing the biopolitical account of human being through which that arbitrary form of political sovereignty was challenged, reveal itself as the central source of a newly insidious imperialism. Simultaneously, this biopolitical account of human being is now being challenged by another, radically hostile account of *what life is* and *what life may become*. Struggling against the sovereign imposition of this liberal biopolitics, we are witnessing in Terror the emergence of an attempt to constitute another way of practising a politics of life. The War on Terror is precisely this, a struggle between competing sovereign impositions over the political constitution of life, each of which in the process do a different form of injustice to the life of human being. It is in this context that the possibility of another way of constituting life politically must be posed. Not another identity politics, masquerading as *the* authentic humanism, which seeks to overcome the resistances and affront of its others by eliminating or excluding their differences, nor by converting difference into identity, or suborning the play of difference to some banal code by which it can be policed. The politics of a life that does not seek security through identity, nor through the development of a world society, the survival of which is fostered by the subordination of all values to the value of security itself. The possibility of a life lived beyond humanity, security and law.

For Deleuze and Guattari the possibility of such an immanently experienced life could only be sought in greater proximity to animal rather than human life. Likewise such a life exists in closer proximity to the domain of war than one of politics. Nomadic life on their account is also the life of the warrior. Not the soldierly life of uniformity and docility with which liberal regimes stamp their armies of subjects in the name of liberal peace, but another, utterly disordered form of life incapable of such uniformity and docility, and which resists the imposition of the terms of such a peace through the use of tactics and strategies deriving from its own peculiar traditions of war. In the following chapters we will pursue the question and problem of the location of Terror in relationship to such a search for an alternative way of conceiving and protecting life. Can the emergence of Terror, of the new and radical strategies that Terror invokes against its liberal enemies, be understood as an outcome of the active desire of life for a form of expression outside biopolitical forms of qualification? In what other ways can we theorise the relations between the advent of Terror and the development of biopolitics and liberal regimes of power? These are the questions to be addressed in the subsequent chapter through the work of another thinker for whom this question and problem has been an abiding concern in very recent years, Jean Baudrillard.

4

Defiant life: the seductions of Terror amid the tyranny of the human

IN THE previous two chapters we examined the roots of the War on Terror in the development of liberal modernity and the roles of disciplinary and biopolitical regimes in constituting it. This is not a war that can be understood in the simplistic terms ascribed to it in many of the critical responses to it to date, where it is largely argued that we are witnessing in it a return of a form of imperialism grounded in an old-fashioned conception of state sovereignty. It is a biopolitical war underwritten by a commitment to the defence of a liberal conception of humanity which exceeds and challenges the boundaries of traditional forms of state sovereignty. The function of sovereign power, here, is in service of the reconstitution and redrawing of a boundary between a biopolitical account of human being and its enemy. This reconstitution and redrawing is, however, only possible in the context of the continuing and more basic functions of biopolitical discourses, agencies and practices. In this sense, it was argued that we have to grasp the interrelation of the biopolitical to the sovereign in Deleuzean terms of the form of a *strategy* where the antagonism between these different forces constitutes itself a productive function in the development of modern biopolitically qualified life forms and processes.

Reconceptualising the War on Terror thus, as biopolitical war, allows us to reproblematise some of its essential features. The biopolitical stakes of this war are embellished particularly in the characterisation of an enemy distinguished in terms of pathology and inhumanity. Liberal political thinkers such as Benjamin Barber attempt to assure us that this is a war with an enemy whose dispositions are 'predominantly the consequence of pathology and yield neither to rational analysis nor understanding' (Barber 2003: 88). Even more viciously and crudely, Jean Bethke Elshtain argues that the perpetrators of Terror are nothing more than a verminous form of life, and that to search for an understanding or explanation for the contemporary resurgence of violent resistance to the global liberal order is to be 'unwilling or unable to peer into the heart of darkness' and recognise the reality of evil (2004: 1–8). The connotation of the terrorist and the animal is a widely perpetrated discursive technique employed throughout literatures responding to the event of 9/11 and the War on Terror. Malise Ruthven, for example, argues that 'terrorism can be likened to a pest or a parasite, such as the mosquito, which needs stagnant waters or a swamp to breed in. Drain the swamp, clear the waters, and the threat will be reduced, if not eliminated' (Ruthven 2004: 25). In contrast, the Foucauldian position which we have constructed here so far, and from which such claims are reproblematised, allows us to view this War on Terror in an inverted light: a war waged not in defence of an essential form of humanity from its pathological, inhuman, or animal other, but a war being waged against the basic conditions for the movement and expression of life. It is, as both Foucault, and Deleuze and Guattari enable us to think and understand, the aleatory, immeasurable, and nomadic character of life itself which is under threat in the context of this biopolitical war without end.

In response to this reproblematisation of the War on Terror we posed the question at the close of the last chapter of whether and how we might rethink and pursue a politics of life which does not fall party to the imperia of biopolitical conceptions of humanity – the politics of a life that does not seek security through identity, nor through the development of a global vision for humanity, the survival of which it seeks to foster by the annihilation of all values except the value of security itself; the possibility of a life lived beyond humanity, security and its limits. From the Deleuzean perspective which we explored in the previous chapter, this became a question of how to deterritorialise life from its colonisation by biopolitical forms. How, otherwise, to reinvest life with its immanent and nomadic potentials? In this chapter I want to push this question a little further through recourse to a philosophy that has often been misconstrued as antithetical to Foucauldian concerns for problems of biopolitics, that of Jean Baudrillard (Hegarty 2004: 92; Gane 2000: 19–20; R. Butler 1999: 5–6). True, Baudrillard did write a vicious critique of Foucault's analytic of power, titled suitably *Forget Foucault* (1987). However the apparent conflicts between them disguise a more mutual concern with issues precisely of the intersections of power, life, and strategy.

The early works of Baudrillard developed indeed a conception of the strategy of power that is very close to that which we have identified with Foucault. For Baudrillard, as for Foucault, what differentiates the strategies of liberal regimes of power from other forms is their assumption of life itself as an organisational model upon which to transform societies. For Foucault, to recall, the strategies of liberal regimes of power function by transforming life into the logistical life of individuated bodies and through the conjugation of logistical life into the biopolitical life of populations. While the tactics of disciplinary power divide, segment and serialise life into logistical life, the strategies of biopower combine, integrate and coordinate the biopolitical life of populations. Likewise for Baudrillard in *The System of Objects*, liberal regimes govern their societies upon a principle of what he calls a 'general strategy of human relations' according to which 'everything has to intercommunicate, everything has to be functional' and consequent upon which there are 'no more secrets, no more mysteries, everything is organized' because power demands a form of 'absolute conductivity in all internal organs' (1999a: 27–9). This 'obsession', as Baudrillard describes it, of liberal regimes with the logistical value of life has obvious similarities to the critiques of liberal regimes developed by both Foucault and Deleuze and Guattari. And indeed, Baudrillard, like those other authors we have addressed in previous chapters, locates the origins of his own account of this 'strategic model' of power in principles deriving from war. As he argues, the strategy of power

> sustains itself by producing wealth **and** poverty, by producing as many dissatisfactions as satisfactions, as much nuisance as 'progress'. Its only logic is to survive and its strategy in this regard is to keep human society out of kilter, in perpetual deficit. We know the system has traditionally and powerfully drawn on the aid of *war* to survive and to revive. Today the mechanisms and functions of war have been integrated into the economic system and the mechanisms of daily life. (1999b: 55)

Remarkably, the text in which Baudrillard develops this argument, *The Consumer Society*, was published in 1970, some years before Foucault made his own seminal arguments on the relations between war and power which we examined in chapter 1. Yet, in spite of the explicit nature of the claim that Baudrillard made on the relation between war and liberal modernity, he pursued the argument no further. Indeed, although Baudrillard has attracted much attention for his comments on the specificity of the Gulf War (Gane 2000: 77–87; Der Derian 1995: 199–204; Genosko 1994: 98–104; Baudrillard 1991), he makes no explicit attempt thereafter to engage with the general theorisation of the relation between war and liberal regimes offered by Foucault or other major contemporaries such as Deleuze and Guattari. Yet, in spite of this fact, Baudrillard has a lot to say to the debate on the problem of war, its relations to life and the development of liberal regimes of power concerned with the discipline, regulation and control of life forms and processes that Foucault as well as Deleuze and Guattari developed in their work. In turn, what Baudrillard has to say on these theoretical problems are of immense importance in the context of a War on Terror in which liberal regimes assure us that it is the life of a common humanity which is at stake against an enemy defined in terms of a pathological inhumanity (Elshtain 2004; Barber 2003).

Baudrillard's critique of the modern development of the 'general strategy of human relations' challenges us to rethink precisely what we understand by concepts and definitions of humanity and life. For the outcome of the development of this general strategy for the establishment of an 'absolute conductivity' within human relations is, Baudrillard argues, a society in which the most essential and definitive capacities of life are outlawed; the capacities to possess a secret, to be obdurately other, or to be obscure. These are, Baudrillard argues, the most basic and irreducible conditions for life, and yet they are, through this creation of a society which searches for the most absolute condition of inter-communication, under threat of extinction. Indeed, he goes further than this on occasions, to argue that these capacities for secrecy and obscurity have already disappeared, and that any theory which seeks to comprehend this strategy must recognise the fact of it already having achieved a victory over these fundamental, but now quaint, qualities of life. The organisation of societies has already crossed a critical threshold of development, he argues, after which we can only struggle to think about the possibility of a retreat to some previous state of affairs in which life was lived differently.

Forcing us to confront the secrecy and obscurity of life in opposition to the relationality and transparency of the human, Baudrillard also forces us to address the status and meaning of terrorist forms of resistance to the imposition of these ideological forms of humanity upon peoples. In existing critical responses to the event of 9/11 and the developing phenomenon of 'international terrorism' from within International Relations there is an overriding observation as to the impossibility of being able to negotiate or have a dialogue with this new enemy which is, it is said, 'beyond deterrence' (Kellner 2002: 158; Freedman 2002: 40). This refusal of 'Terror' to offer a rationally realisable or even political set of demands for their enemies to barter with is held up as the defining feature of their pathology and inhumanity. Baudrillard's thesis is quite the opposite. Faced with a form of power the strategy of which functions by bringing bodies into relation and forcing them to communicate, Terror, he argues, responds with a strategy of no negotiation, and with the outright refusal of communication. Faced with the biopower of liberal regimes the object of which is the destruction of the secrecy and obscurity of life itself, Terror responds by attempting to reclaim that secrecy and obscurity as strategy. The integrity of this Terror, he argues, is to be located in its attempt to defend life against the life-governing techniques of liberal regimes. This is the main thesis of Baudrillard in respect of the existence and late modern development of the contemporary form of war-making described as Terror.

In conceiving Terror as a response to the biopower of liberal regimes, Baudrillard is also concerned, then, to conceive it is as a form of strategy. For Foucault as well as Deleuze and Guattari, strategy is, on the whole, a concept to be associated with the ways in which power suborns life to its own ends. Baudrillard, in contrast, remains fairly committed to the idea of and potential for a counter-strategy to power, albeit a strategy which breaks irredeemably with traditional forms of social strategy governed by political ends. Indeed much of his work is dedicated toward a critique of the rational-calculative strategies with which traditional forms of social struggles, particularly class-based struggles have attempted to resist powers of state and capital. In a similar fashion to his contemporaries he conceives the contemporary task of subverting power to be bound up with a need to take account of the ways in which the traditional formulations of social strategies of resistance to power are themselves effectively disabled by the degree to which they are shaped by the needs and requirements of liberal regimes. He argues that in order to subvert the radically intercommunicative and infrastructural organisation of liberal regimes it is necessary to develop modes of thought that adopt a different disposition to the problem of power from that of traditional social strategic thought. In this sense, the question that Baudrillard poses of 'strategy' is basically consistent with that posed by Deleuze and Guattari in respect to life. As Deleuze and Guattari asked whether there is not a form of life that escapes the codification and appropriative mechanisms of liberal regimes of power, so Baudrillard asks whether there are ways of subverting liberal regimes that can be differentiated from the forms of strategic rationality that have traditionally defined the ways in which power has been socially contested. As he argues:

> a mistake concerning strategy is a serious matter. All the movements which only bet on liberation, emancipation, the resurrection of the subject of history, of the group, of speech as a raising of consciousness, indeed of a 'seizure of the unconscious' of subjects and of the masses, do not see that they are acting in accordance with the system, whose imperative today is the over-production and regeneration of meaning and speech. (1983: 109)

Ultimately, then, the argument to be made in this chapter is that Baudrillard urges us to interpret the development of Terror in recent years not simply as an aberration of humanity, but as a shift in strategies dedicated to the defence of the integrity of life against its biopolitical subjugation. In this context we can develop Baudrillard's account of the strategy of seduction as a means with which to interrogate the logic of Terror.

The principles upon which he develops his account of the strategy of seduction arise out of a markedly different attempt to resolve the problem of life's seizure by biopower to those developed by Deleuze and Guattari as well as Foucault. In this chapter we can both use Baudrillard to make sense of the phenomenon of Terror and the importance of the event of 9/11 – in a way that we would struggle to through the lenses offered by those other authors – as well as to differentiate his thinking concerning the relations between war, liberal strategies, and life from them. To do this we have to locate the development of Terror and its counter-strategy of seduction in the context of the crisis of social strategy which Baudrillard detects and details as a defining feature of the global era.

Liberalism, strategy, humanity

To understand the strategy of Terror as seduction we have to locate it as a response to the declining efficacy of more traditional methods of political resistance. The increasing liberalisation of global power relations is crucial to such an understanding. Baudrillard argues that the globalisation of societies has resulted not simply from the decline in the traditional powers of nation-states, but more crucially as the result of a shift in strategies of social control toward methods which now exceed the traditional state-form. In this context the question of how regimes of power deal with and respond to the problem of social resistance is, Baudrillard thinks, important. Traditionally, throughout the modern era, segments of societies fought against their state representatives for more egalitarian and democratic social systems involving greater equalisation of power relations. The entire history of class-based forms of struggle and the various historical revolutions such struggle initiated is only understandable in the context of that demand for greater equality. State powers, in turn, sought traditionally to defend their legitimacy by regulating the economic inequalities and political contradictions of society. In *The Consumer Society* as well as throughout much of his later work, Baudrillard argues that the decline in the traditional powers of nation-states, and their relative foundations in the administration of justice and law, has occurred as a result of the emergence of a much more refined and insidious method of social control. Traditionally, he argues, the legitimacy of modern regimes of power was based on their ability to at least offer the discursive possibility of a form of society in which all power relations would be equalised and all political struggles ended. The legitimacy of the modern nation-state itself was tied to the ideal of a nation to which it was the task of the state to give transparent representation. Even if the distribution of power was perceived to be unequal and unfair, modern societies remained founded for a long period of their history on the belief that it would at a certain historical point of departure become possible to eradicate those inequalities. The decline of the nation-state and the crisis in traditional modernist ideals about the possibilities of politics arises, Baudrillard argues, not simply because those ideals were wrong or ill-founded in any essential sense, but because regimes of power have abandoned the discourse of social equality in favour of a much more effective strategy. The legitimacy of expressly liberal regimes of power, he argues, depends now on their capacity to secure *difference* rather than equality (Baudrillard 1999b: 94). And this, he argues, is to be understood as a strategic shift in the organisation of power rather than an emancipative shift in knowledge about the diversity of power relations, as has often been argued from more conventional perspectives (classically, for example, in Laclau and Mouffe 1986).

This has significant implications, Baudrillard argues, for how we understand the changing character of political resistance in a postmodern and globalised age. From at least the late 1960s onwards, the characteristics of the ways in which societies resist the regimes they are subject to have undergone substantial change. The class struggles of the high-modern era were based upon the ideology of a contradictory clash of forces in which it was necessary for the impoverished masses to seize control of the state in order to annihilate their class enemy. In recent decades, however, that ideology of dialectical contradiction, so historically powerful, has been displaced by a new ideology of difference. Struggles for sexual liberation, for the emancipation of women and promotion of feminist agendas, as well as for a more multi-cultural society respectful of racial identity and tolerant of different religions have become the new norm. Yet, rather than reading these developments, as many do, as progressive shifts in the character of political struggle, Baudrillard identifies in them the emergence of new strategies of control. Whereas the class war was a struggle of contradictory forces in which the victory of one set of antagonists spelt the defeat of the other, the new forms of struggle are constitutive, he argues, of a new order in which the identities of resistant subjectivities circulate within a system in which there are no distinctions of absolute opposition, only bodies differentiated according to their position within that circulatory system. This is because, he argues, liberalism is a strategy which systematically aims at the production of differences 'in accordance with an order which integrates them all as identifying signs', thus annulling the organisation of contradictions and essential antagonisms which defined more traditionally modern forms of society. According to Baudrillard's analysis, then, the liberalisation of global power relations signifies the 'absorption' of the traditional social logic of contradiction, and represents a defining achievement in the advance of liberalism's strategy of power (Baudrillard 1975: 126). It is as a result of this shift, he argues, that it is necessary to rethink the ways in which we engage with this strategy, if, that is, we are still interested in powerfully challenging it (1983: 98–105).

Foucault's analysis of the development of biopolitics arrived, in fact, at similar conclusions. The growth of a human rights culture in which 'the "right" to life, to one's body, to health, to happiness, to the satisfaction of needs ... the "right" to rediscover what one is and all that one can be' is a product, Foucault argued, of the emergence of biopolitical regimes of power which function through the seizure and control of life rather than its negation (1990: 145). It is true that in his participation in particular political struggles, Foucault appeared to endorse a strategic use of human rights discourse and legislation (2001c). In various interviews he outlined ways in which liberal subjects might strategically intervene in the constitution of their identities as bearers of the right to life, particularly in relationship to issues of identity based on claims to sexuality (Simons 1995: 96–9). However, the fundamental argument which emerges from *The History of Sexuality* in particular is to the effect that forms of resistance which assume human life as their own political object for defence and development, as human rights-based forms of struggle do, are explicable only in the context of the development of such regimes and their increasing control and command over life. The right to express a sexuality, to practise a particular religion, or to belong to a specific race and culture, are all forms of empowerment constituted within the development of liberal biopolitical regimes of governance concerned with the codification of what life is and what life may become (Cruikshank 1999). Now, Baudrillard's analysis of this set of developments, while different to Foucault's in crucial degrees and respects, is nevertheless situated within a biopolitical framework in which power's control and command over life is dependent upon its capacity to enable life as opposed to disable life. In terms very close to those of Foucault's, Baudrillard argues in his early work *Symbolic Exchange and Death*, that, 'the power of the master *always* primarily derives from suspension of death. Power is therefore never, contrary to what we might imagine, the power of putting to death, but exactly the opposite, that of allowing to live – a life that the slave lacks the power to give' (1999c: 40).

Yet, this proximity of the positions occupied by Baudrillard and Foucault in the mid-1970s on the question of power, was significantly altered by the publication of Baudrillard's notorious *Forget Foucault* as well as *Fatal Strategies*. Published at a time when Foucault's reputation in France was at a premium, these texts led to the virtual exclusion of Baudrillard from the French academic establishment of the period. In any case, his influence and standing was minor in comparison to Foucault at this point. *The Consumer Society* was yet to be translated into English, and he was not to recover any major influence until the 1980s (Gane 2000: 1). Baudrillard's disagreement with Foucault was based not so much on the question of the relations between liberal regimes of power and life which they essentially shared, but on the question of how to resist power once its relation to life and productive character is recognised and specified (1990: 78–9). For Foucault, to recall, the recognition that the strategy of power is productive rather than repressive of life led to the conclusion that power achieves an 'omnipresence' throughout social relations by organising the emergence of life-affirmative actions and thoughts which assume the form of resistance (1990: 92–6). Rather than viewing resistance in terms of an irruption of some vital force in antagonism with a repressive regime of power, it is necessary, he argued, to view power itself as a vital system that organises the relations between resistance and power in a productive manner. This led Foucault to argue that to resist liberal regimes of power through the assertion of the right to life is always necessarily in some way or other to be complicit with the (re)production of biopolitical power relations (1990: 94–5).

Baudrillard certainly recognises the same problematic. He argues that what is distinct about the liberal approach to the problem of power is its explicit understanding of the strategic benefits of being able to secure the practice of resistance as a search for life-affirmative forms of difference. This is evident, for example, in the work of a key liberal thinker such as John Stuart Mill for whom the development of a society in which subjects are given the freedom to distinguish themselves on grounds of their different lifestyles and life choices is a building block for a better ordered and more securely integrated society (Baudrillard 1999a: 141). Beyond that, Baudrillard also argues more forcefully that a principle of transgression and resistance is central to the ways in which liberal societies transform themselves and achieve orderly processes of change. This is identifiable, he argues, as early as Mandeville's suggestion in the eighteenth century that liberal societies can achieve order not by securing the morality or positive aspects of their value systems, but by providing space for the exercise of transgression (Baudrillard 1999c: 98; Mandeville 1962).

Foucault's response to this problem of liberal regimes of power that function by making the production of life itself an operative principle for the reproduction of power relations was, as we have already discussed in the previous chapter, fairly ineffable. Foucault provides scarce means to imagine or construe what life might actually be or become outside of liberal regimes of power that command and control life to a degree of 'omnipresence' (1990: 93). In the context of this failure, Deleuze and Guattari's radical theorisation of the nomadic potentialities of life for the deterritorialisation of power was our focus in the previous chapter. Deleuze and Guattari sought to conceive how life, in spite of liberal regimes' attempts to command and control its processes of becoming, nevertheless always manages to escape power's strategy, producing and proliferating in different ways beyond such regimes' calculations as to how life ought to be made. Baudrillard's response to this problem of liberal regimes' command of life is, in contrast, of another order entirely. Rather than attempt to radicalise life's productive capacities in antagonism with liberal regimes' attempts to command and control it in the terms that Deleuze and Guattari argue for, Baudrillard attempts to problematise the very notion of life's productivity itself. If, he argues, the strategy of liberal regimes operates upon a principle of the production and enablement of life, then an intelligent response to that strategy must be based upon the subversion of the law of the productivity of life itself through which biopolitical power relations are reproduced. Not through an increase in the vitality of the forms of life that liberal regimes of power attempt to command, but by a subversion of the ideal of vitality itself. Herein lies the key to Baudrillard's conception of a counter-strategy of seduction which he, in turn, identifies with the development of a form of terrorism, culminating in the attack on the World Trade Center of 9/11, and which he argues has effectively turned upside-down 'the whole play of history and power relations' (2003: 149). To comprehend the efficacy of Terror and the nature of its counter-strategy it is imperative, he argues, that we grasp how it subverts as he describes it, 'the rules of the game' by shifting the terrain of struggle 'into the sphere of the symbolic, where the rule is that of defiance, reversion and outbidding' (2003:

151, 154). In doing so we can identify, he argues, a strategic logic to Terror oriented to the defence of the most basic conditions for life over and against the accusations of nihilism, pathology and irrationality ascribed to it in the main-stay of critical responses to the World Trade Center attack and the ensuing conflict. In turn we can also mount a defence of Baudrillard's own theorisation of power and its relations to life against the accusations of nihilism and irra-tionality ascribed to it in superficial responses to his work (for example Norris 2000a: 2; Norris 2000b: 155–8).

Terror, life, pathology

In order to grasp the subversive efficacy of Terror, Baudrillard argues that we have to contrast it with more moribund traditional forms of subversion. Traditionally, social movements have attempted to subvert power by trans-gressing it. The concept of 'the social' itself refers in the abstract to that category which has been called upon, at least ever since Rousseau, to resist and transgress power through producing and building its own idealised forms of counter-subjectivity. Through the identification and pursuit of its foundational needs and desires the social has acted as the motor of political history, transgressing the law with a view to transforming the law, in the name of some future perfected ideal of what society can become (R. Butler 1999: 58–63; Baudrillard 1983: 17). That tradition of the social as the productive subject of transgression is, Baudrillard argues, now defunct. What distinguishes Terror is its contrast with the technique of transgression, its constitution of a form of life which exists outside of history, its lack of an ideology, its refusal of productivity, and its disinterest in any ability to transform the organisation of societies. Terror func-tions as a subversion of the law instead by refusing the rules of this traditional game. The rules, that is, of transgression, of transformation, and of productiv-ity. As he puts it:

> Terror against terror, there is no more ideology behind this. One is, from this point forward, far beyond ideology and politics. No ideology, no cause – not even the Islamic one – can explain the energy that feeds terror. It no longer aims at transforming the world. Like heresies in more ancient times, it aims at radicalising the world through sacrifice, while the system aims at realizing the world by force. (2003: 151)

What renders Terror 'radical' in doing so is, Baudrillard argues, its underlying rejection of all the cardinal principles of strategic action. Strategy is, as we have already discussed, traditionally understood as the calculation of means to ends. Action only has a strategic value if it can be calculated in subordination to some political end that is being achieved in its execution. Terror, in contrast, Baudrillard argues, is devoid of utility. What horrifies the liberal conscience when faced with the spectre of Terror is its absolute negation of the idea that death can only have a value if it can be understood to be useful in one way or another to the improvement of life. Terror does not kill in pursuit of some better life, nor does it embrace death for death's sake, for that would still render it subject to the law of use value, but enacts a symbolic death given only as sacrifice. This is what Baudrillard believes defines the intuitive genius of the strategy of Terror; its refusal of the limits through and within which life has traditionally been strategised. Here, then, Baudrillard argues that Terror is effective in so far as it enacts a strategy located in the order of what he first described as 'symbolic exchange' (1999c). Symbolic exchange, he argues, is effective as strategy in so far as it challenges power by returning to it its own logic, thus effectively reciprocating with it (Cook 1995: 150). Rather than remaining within the rules of the game in which subversion must always be committed to in the form of some kind of transgressive counter-communication with power, some act of resistance to power in production of another potential counter-subjectivity, Terror obeys the desire of the empowered subject which reigns over it. Recognising that it is dealing with a regime the power of which depends upon the conditioning of life to enter into the strategic game of contesting its status as object, constituting itself as a subject, Terror enacts the life of the object.

Now there are several objections that can be made to such an account of Terror as a strategy divested of politics and the quest for subjectivity. One is that it contrasts with the most standard accounts of Terror as an expression of the pursuit of what Malise Ruthven has described as a 'fury for God' (2004). Ruthven argues that the perpetrators of the contemporary form of Terror are profoundly ideologically and politically driven. Ruthven takes the 'Islamic' motivations of contemporary expressions of Terror very seriously. In doing so, he does not argue that the 9/11 attack and the ensuing war against the liberal West can be understood as a genuine expression of the Islamic religion. Rather, he accounts for Terror as an expression of a hybrid and essentially politically motivated bastardisation of Islamic beliefs and writings. Most fundamentally he argues that the use of terrorism has a specific tactical utility in so far as it is designed to provoke the liberal West to respond on a massive scale against the Islamic world and thus radicalise the sense of alienation and hatred of Islamic populations for the perpetrators of violence against them (Ruthven 2004: 101–2). This tactical deployment of terrorism has its antecedents, Ruthven argues, in the development of revolutionary strains of anarchism within the modern West (2004: 91). Through the work of militant Islamic scholars such as Sayyid Qutb, modern and secular revolutionary ideas about the use of terrorism gradually became conflated with specific and idiosyncratic readings of classical Islamic works to proffer, he argues, a fanatical ideology according to which suicide becomes construed as a divinely ordained but nevertheless tactical weapon of political struggle (2004: 72–97). Indeed, if we examine the discourse of the proponents of terrorism contemporarily it is not difficult to identify what could otherwise be described as a political programme. The statements of Osama bin Laden released to the world's media have consistently been characterised with demands for the withdrawal of United States military forces from Saudi Arabia, with demands for the provision of security to the Palestinian people, and more ambiguously and problematically, for the withdrawal of the West itself from the whole of the Middle East.

Baudrillard's approach is not to deny that these political claims exist, nor that the individuals and groups involved don't have some sense of a political, ideologically driven mission. What he argues is that these discourses and motivations create what is in effect an 'illusion' of a confrontation and possibility of a political solution between Western and Islamic worlds (Baudrillard 2003: 152). Both the United States and Islam itself are, he argues, mere 'spectres' which generate this illusion of a political struggle. Beyond this illusory idiom of political conflict there resides a form of agency, he argues, deeper and more profound than the individuals and groups involved, deeper and more profound than the states and societies involved, deeper and more profound than any civilisation or culture, more profound than the forms of agency conferred on peoples by the forces of religion. That is, the agency of life itself: a life rooted in the condition of an antagonism now threatened by this phenomenon of liberal regimes of power which believe themselves capable of monopolising their claims to be able to answer the questions of what life is and what life may become on a global basis, and secure the conditions upon which life gives its own answers in response to those questions globally too; and being able to root out the source of all manifestations of antagonism, and striate life on a planetary scale accordingly under conditions of what it calls the law of humanity. There is much more at stake in this conflict, then, if we believe Baudrillard, than religion and politics. Terror expresses an irreducible antagonism that neither the United States nor Islam itself is capable of generating. As he argues, 'if Islam dominated the world, terrorism would rise against Islam. It is the very world itself that resists globalization' (2003: 152). The political discourses which cloak the expression of Terror contemporarily are superfluous when compared to their origins in an antagonism as deeply rooted as life itself.

Terror is radical, for Baudrillard then, because it would seem to involve the recovery of an ability to offer a meaningful challenge to and defiance of modern, Western, and moreover, liberal values. And the strength of this challenge resides not in its political claims, but in its refusal of politics. Now what is striking about this depiction of Terror as a strategy divested of any coherent desire for subjectivity, absent of any transformational vision for society which he offers us, is its proximity to the condition which has led some liberal theorists of International Relations to label movements such as Al Qaeda as brutal and inhumane. Jean Bethke Elshtain, in her widely acclaimed *Just War against Terror*, argues for example that Al Qaeda are fanatics 'that have lost the capacity for argument that entertains multiple possibilities' (2003: 154). It is this condition of the absence of the ability to reason which means that the only viable response to Terror, from Elshtain's point of view, is 'interdiction and self-defence' (2003: 154). There is no point, Elshtain argues, in attempting to seek out rationalisations, underlying causes or explanations for terrorist action. The only viable course of action in the short term is to stop Terror by interrupting it 'in all its aspects', and in the long term by 'building up secure civil infrastructures (2003: 154). If terrorist groups such as Al Qaeda were to articulate some yearning for a political subjectivity, one could reason and negotiate with it. Instead, Terror exhibits a 'violence that kills politics' and which in turn disables any possibility for argument or persuasion (Elshtain 2003: 152).

Other critical respondents to the 9/11 attack have remonstrated with this type of perspective developed by Elshtain. Many have argued and will continue to argue that this view of terrorism as a threat bereft of a political will, of reason, or indeed of social and historical causes, is entirely wrong. Judith Butler, for example, argues in her recent work *Precarious Life* that this manner of telling the story of 9/11 which Elshtain pursues, by starting from the event of the attack itself, and excluding the prehistory of imperial subjugation of Islamic peoples by the United States and other liberal regimes as a source of explanation for the attack, is an ethically irresponsible and strategically ineffective form of response. Instead, she argues, 'we can say, and ought to, that US imperialism is a necessary condition for the attacks on the United States, that these attacks would be impossible without the horizon of imperialism within which they occur' (2004: 11). To understand Terror, we have to grasp and detail the historical, social and political conditions upon which the individual perpetrators of terrorism 'are formed, and we would be making a mistake if we reduced their actions to purely self-generated acts of will or symptoms of individual pathology or evil' (Butler 2004: 15). In turn, if we can do so, there remains the possibility that we might escape the 'narrative perspective of US unilateralism' which configures the diagnosis offered by theorists such as Elsthain, in order that we might alternatively 'consider the ways in which our lives are profoundly implicated in the lives of others' (Butler 2004: 7).

Butler's argument is certainly an appealing one when set against the backdrop of the mainstay of responses to the attack that have emerged from the United States since 9/11. The advent of Terror entails, she argues in contrast with Elshtain, its own history, its own peculiar set of political and social conditions, which in turn can be examined in order to explain it. There is a rational basis to the use of terrorism currently explained by the history of imperial subjugation of Muslim populations by the United States and other liberal regimes. And in its continued use of military violence against Muslim societies, the United States is she argues 'offering a breeding ground for new waves of young Muslims to join terrorist organizations' (2004: 17). Terror breeds, she argues, in agreement with other critics of the militarised response to 9/11 such as Mary Kaldor, in terrains where 'becoming a criminal or joining a paramilitary group is literally the only opportunity for unemployed young men lacking formal education' (Kaldor quoted in Butler 2004: 11–12). In turn the inference is that a strategy to end Terror must provide the 'formal education' and other life chances by which the forms of life that manifest Terror can be bred differently.

Butler's previous works such as *The Psychic Life of Power* and *Subjects of Desire* (Butler 1997; 1999) have won acclaim for their utilisation of Foucault as a resource from which to powerfully broach major philosophical and political questions (Gabardi 2001: 14; Žižek 2000: 253). And *Precarious Life* itself does draw on Foucault to attempt to rethink the problem of sovereignty in the context of the War on Terror (2004: 51–4). Yet, set in context of Butler's profound theoretical debt to Foucault, her recourse to the concept of the 'breeding ground' as an explanation for terrorism is disappointing. Foucault's own biopolitical analysis of liberal regimes of power was developed, as we have already encountered, to problematise the discursive framework and regimes of power within which life comes to be conceived as amenable to the techniques of conditioning, shaping and enablement which are otherwise captured so acutely in this concept of a life which is 'bred', and which Butler would have us accept as the main precondition from which to understand the life that manifests Terror. Such a discursive framework for the comprehension of Terror is one that rationalises the development of the life of Terror in accordance with its conditioning by a lack of subjectivity. The life which feeds on the breeding grounds Butler depicts is a life born of insufficiency, which could have been bred differently, but which exposed to a particular set of social and political conditions falls into the vagaries of Terror as the only means possible by which to articulate its desire to fulfil the conditions for political subjectivity. The argument offered by Butler, then, is that Terror is a 'weapon of the weak', born of a desperation and plight contingent upon its exposure to a lack of subjectivity.

In contrast, Baudrillard's account of the radicalism of Terror is, if anything, closer to Elshtain's account of it as pathology and evil. Nevertheless, in being so, it is also a much more Foucauldian account of Terror than Butler's or any of the other attempts to frame the life of Terror within a discourse of lack. For Elshtain, of course, the pathology of Terror is likewise born of a failing or an inability. The terrorist has as she argues '*lost* the capacity for argument that entertains multiple possibilities' (2003: 154). For Baudrillard, in contrast, the pathology and indeed evil of Terror is a capacity which the life of Terror has gained or assumed. Yet this becoming pathological and evil of life is both strategic and necessary, he thinks, in the context of a world governed by a strategy of power which functions by attempting to outlaw the condition of pathology and evil itself. When the organisation of power is defined by the naïve belief in an ability to secure the conditions for the development of the 'good life' bereft of any relation to evil, in the suffocating condition of a peace established in the belief that it is possible to outlaw war, in the endurance of an attempt to secure the health of the species in the belief that it is possible to remove altogether life's pathologies, then it is, Baudrillard believes, the task of life itself to recover its capacity for evil, pathology, and war. Set in such a biopolitical context of the problem of a regime of power and a form of strategy which functions through the absorption of life's most essential properties, Baudrillard's account of Terror as counter-strategy must be understood as a forthright attempt to answer some quintessential Foucauldian problems. What form does life take when its own conditions of existence are effectively outlawed by a regime of power that governs through the administration of life? What can and might life become when it is subject to a rule of measure which seeks to govern its own peculiar ways of becoming? These are the questions which lie at the root of Baudrillard's account of Terror as counter-strategy. As such Baudrillard depicts Terror not as a 'weapon of the weak' born of the desperation of depravity or ill-breeding but as a weapon 'of the rich'. Such exponents of Terror have, he argues 'become rich (and they have all the means) while wishing for our defeat. Of course, according to our value system, they cheat, since it's not fair play to put one's own death at stake. But they do not care, and the new rules of the game no longer belong to us' (Baudrillard 2003: 157).

Terror as defiant life

The subversive efficacy of Terror resides, Baudrillard thinks, in its rejection of the very principles of subversion which inform not only the traditions of class-based struggle but, as importantly, those accounts of the potential for subversion of biopolitical governance within the more steadfastly Foucauldian tradition itself. In this context Baudrillard draws not only Foucault into his sights, but Deleuze and Guattari as well. Indeed in developing his account of Terror as a strategy for countering the biopolitical colonisation of life Baudrillard is keen to differentiate it directly from Deleuze and Guattari's theorisation of the deterritorialising desires of nomadic life. The strategy of Terror is based, Baudrillard argues, on the outright refusal of the entire logos of desire, claiming instead that while 'only the subject desires, only the object seduces' (1990: 111). Terror is the strategy of a protagonist, Baudrillard believes, which rather than suborning itself to the productivity of its own desires and the pursuit of new forms of nomadic subjectivity constituted through the following of its own life-giving desires, plays on its antagonist – a subject – with the aim of drawing out and fulfilling the most definitive desire of that antagonist. Seduction functions as strategy through the abnegation of one's own productive desire in order to render subject the desire of one's enemy which without that abnegation of self could not be fulfilled and yet which in its fulfilment destroys the enemy's own conditions of subjectivity. That basic desire is, Baudrillard argues, the desire of the subject for its own death, or suicide.

As forbidding as it might at first seem, we can employ this argument directly to make sense of how Terror functions strategically in the context of the War on Terror. Many have remarked upon the fact that the 9/11 attack on the World Trade Center which formally instigated the war was an event which had already found powerful representation in the Western media prior to its occurrence. Slavoj Žižek, for example, observed how prior to the event of 9/11 the media in the United States were not only 'bombarding us all the time with talk about the terrorist threat' but were representing its possibility for consumption and fantasy in Hollywood films such as *Escape from New York* and *Independence Day* – to the point where Žižek thinks it fair to argue that on that balmy morning in New York 'America got what it fantasized about, and this was the greatest surprise' (Žižek 2003: 132). To understand the power of the attack upon the society of the United States and that of liberal societies more generally, Žižek's point is, we have to recognise the ways in which it played upon not simply a fear of terrorism, but an active desire for this spectacular act of destruction, an act which had found full representation in American film, and which was in effect a fantasy of American society for its own destruction.

But what 'America got' on that morning was something much more profound than simply a spectacularly violent attack upon one of its most iconic symbols, the Twin Towers. What 'America got' was more than that, it was confirmation of the existence of a type of enemy which it had imagined, conjured with, and feared the possibility of for many years. That enemy was, variably, the animal, the pathological individual, the harbinger of evil, the irra-tional fanatic, a form of life so inhuman it could not be defended against. Of course, this was not the first time that the United States had thought itself to be pitched in a war of theological importance and character. The discourse of the Cold War was saturated with depictions of a communist enemy deemed variably to be 'barbaric', 'pathological' or 'evil' (Campbell 1998: 169–98). Yet what distinguishes the strategy of Terror today, Baudrillard believes, is its deliberate invocation of this discourse. The characterisation of the threat of the Soviet Union and broader communist movements that defined the Cold War as a force of 'evil' was always an absurd one given the pronounced modern and secular character of the political struggle and opposed regimes involved. In essence the Soviet Union was competing with the United States in an argument as to which regime could give the most authentic representation to secular modern and humanist political struggles. Which of these two regimes could lay the greater claim to be the expression of modern, secular, humanist ideals? In this context of what was in essence a shared discourse of modernity, secularity, and human-ity, it could only be through an immense effort that the United States was able to construct its enemy as pathological or evil. David Campbell's seminal study of the strategies of discursive construction through which the United States deployed discourses of pathology and evil to vilify its enemy and secure the boundary between the identity of American society and its other has demonstrated precisely this with alacrity (Campbell 1998). Yet, the strategy of Terror functions very differently. In contrast with the threat of communism and the Soviet Union, posited as it was through a rival claim of access to modernity and its political truths, Terror threatens the United States, and other liberal societies, through its deliberate refusal of the modern game of political truth saying. It actively and wilfully engages its construction as evil, pathological and irrational. It invites and confirms this depiction because it knows and understands that what this form of regime and society which it seeks to defy is endangered by most, and which paradoxically it cannot help but fantasise about the existence of, is an enemy which subverts the limits of its means for the comprehension of life itself. The extent of this danger goes way beyond the simple fact that the War on Terror is a war of states against non-state actors with whom a regular peace settlement would be difficult to achieve. What differentiates the War on Terror from all previous wars is the refusal of Terror of any political stakes through which a settlement with it could be achieved. Its inhumanity resides in its obscurity rather than its desire for subjectivity.

This 'inhumanity' is functioning strategically today in so far as it is forcing the United States and its allies to themselves sacrifice the very principles of humanity which they claim to be concerned with defending. The creation of the US Patriot Act after 9/11 and the development of the Domestic Security Enhancement Act in the US, involve the sacrifice of the human rights and freedoms which liberal societies and regimes have traditionally been defined in accordance with. Guilt by association, indefinite detention, and the power to arrest and search in secret are all practices that we would ordinarily associate with what would otherwise be described as an 'illiberal' form of society (Cole 2003: 58–71). And this shift is occurring in the context of a war against an enemy whose own 'inhumanity' is defined by its purported secrecy and obscurity over and against the democratically representative and transparent qualities of supposedly more humane regimes. In this situation, where the inhumanity and evil of an enemy is based upon its rejection of liberal humanist conceptions of life, so the creeping development of liberal regimes toward evermore illiberal social forms can only be understood in terms of an outcome of victory. The strategy of Terror functions, Baudrillard claims, by seducing its enemy to effectively destroy its own conditions of existence.

The catastrophe of humanity

Understood thus, the War on Terror is not reducible from Baudrillard's perspective to a struggle over how to live the 'good life', or how to achieve and then suspend eternally a social state in which the human species itself can be secured. It is not that one should side with these other inhuman forces called Terror for the sake of the belief that they represent some more preferable alternative way of life or model of society. Instead the War on Terror and the violence it entails is to be understood as the necessary result of not just the naïvety but the essentially immoral purpose of a regime of power which has attempted to exterminate the moral principle of evil itself from the 'tiniest crevices' of its social order (Baudrillard 2004: 106–7). Quoting Montaigne to the effect that 'if we eliminated evil in Man we would destroy the fundamental conditions of life' (2004: 110), Baudrillard locates in the event of 9/11 the secretion of an enemy which the imperia of the idea of humanity, served by the various liberal regimes of power which have carried it forward historically and which the United States now finds itself the most aggressive subject of, was destined to produce. Setting itself the absurd task of securing a 'hegemony of the Good' (2004: 107), the liberal humanist imagination is now, it would seem, forced to come to terms with the irreducibility of the existence of evil in the world. No society can survive, Baudrillard argues, without in some respect allowing for the radical opposition of a rival system of value. The perversity of the development of liberal modernity, empowered so forcefully by its humanist imagination, is the extremity with which it has pursued that possibility of the extinction of evil. The pathology of Terror in this context is, Baudrillard argues, the responsibility of the system itself. After 9/11, it is as if we can breathe again in the knowledge that the moral integrity of the world, its essentially Manichean foundations, subsists. At the same time, the recognition of the morally reconstitutive function of Terror in defiant protection of what life in its essence is, does not forbid us from recognising it as the catastrophe of immorality that it is for liberal modernity. As Baudrillard states:

> any structure that hunts down, expels or exorcises its negative elements risks a catastrophe caused by a thoroughgoing backlash, just as any organism that hunts down and eliminates its germs, bacteria, parasites or other biological antagonists risks metastasis and cancer – in other words, it is threatened by a voracious positivity of its own cells, or in the viral context, by the prospect of being devoured by its own – now unemployed – antibodies. (1999d: 106)

The question of agency and strategy in this context, then, is very complex. On the one hand it makes no sense to attempt to account for the event of 9/11 simply in terms of a conscious strategy developed and pursued by the individuals or groups involved against an innocent society and regime. Nor can it be understood simply as a result of a wicked project dedicated to the imperial subjugation and exploitation of another innocent people. What this event signifies instead is something like a 'deep complicity' in the relations between liberal regimes and the Terror with which they are now faced (Baudrillard 2003: 150). This complicity signifies life's own strategy of subversion against any given society or subjectivity that attempts to foster its own hegemonic account of what life is or what life may become. The individuals and groups involved in this event are not as Elshtain would have us believe the source of a pathological violence which knows nothing of the 'dignity' of human life (Elshtain 2004: 195). Rather, those individuals and groups are the *cipher* of a pathology which through the use of a violence which is itself immoral, is serving to restore life to a more morally integral state. This pathology arises neither from a fall nor from the incapacity of life to achieve humanity. It emerges in the form of something closer to a secretion of life endangered by its biopolitical subjugation to this anthropocentric force we call humanity. In this sense what Baudrillard is doing is not seeking to praise Terror as an effective form of political action. What he challenges us with is a view of Terror as a counter-strategy of life itself to conditions of a form of humanity which has overreached its own boundaries of development. There is an immorality, he argues, to this biopolitical domination of prevailing conceptions of what life is and what life may become by Western, and more acutely liberal, conceptions of humanity. In this context of biopolitical domination, life itself revolts, and it is in the immorality of Terror that this revolt finds its expression.

Given that in examining Terror, Baudrillard challenges us to reconceive it as, essentially, an affirmation of life rather than simply an abnegation of humanity, so we must recognise Baudrillard as an affirmative thinker. This will no doubt enrage many of his detractors who identify in his thought a form of errant postmodern nihilism (for example Kellner 1995) or simply 'irrationalism' (Norris 2000a: 2). Such accusations, founded as they are on the trodden-to-death grounds of debates surrounding postmodernism, the supposed relativity of truth, and the crisis in modernist social and political values, are not worth recuperating wholesale, and the defence of Baudrillard in regard to these debates could as well be made of Nietzsche or many of the other sources that the regime of enlightenment's hawks are inclined to target. Yet, it must be made clear that Baudrillard's analysis of the conditions of the War on Terror, an analysis which is fully consistent with the broader development of his larger works from its origins in texts such as *Symbolic Exchange and Death*, is founded in a commitment to a concept of truth as a condition for the creation and sustenance of relations between living beings which is stronger than the conception of truth which any of modernity's more steadfastly humanist traditions have ever been able to produce or secure.

The truth about life, Baudrillard argues, is that which cannot be said, that which is secret, and which defends its secrecy at all costs. And this is the form of truth which he argues is imperilled and at stake, as well as enacting its defence, in this War on Terror – a truth about life which comes up against the ever encroaching truth of the human, which those defenders of the 'unfinished project of modernity' such as Christopher Norris still seek to propagate, a form of truth which is always a declared truth, which can be known, revealed and made the 'basis of shared understanding or common humanity' (Norris 2000a: 30). Humanists such as Norris rally against Baudrillard and other anti-humanist thinkers because they believe erroneously that to attempt to think truth as anything other than a knowable or potentially transparent quality is to forbid the possibility of a world involving shared forms of understanding. Yet for Baudrillard, the secretive quality of truth is precisely that which 'circulates through and traverses everything that can be said, just as seduction flows beneath the obscenity of speech. It is the opposite of communication, and yet it can be shared. The secret maintains its power only at the price of remaining unspoken, just as seduction operates only because never spoken nor intended' (1990: 79). A declared truth such as the truth of the human always necessarily is, always also is a divisive truth, the manifestation of which announces a temporality of conflict because agreement with it depends upon recognition of its credibility, a credibility which by its nature is open to contestation. Liberal modernity is the narrative unfolding of that time, a time of struggle for the propagation and security of the conditions of human truth over and against any and every other account of what life is or may become. Based in a fundamentalist view of the world whereby the continuance of conflict in the world is itself just a residual product of the fact that certain groups and individuals remain 'prevent[ed] from perceiving their common humanity' (Norris 2000a: 41), liberal extremists like Norris commit themselves ever more forcefully to the project of the eradication of all cultural and socially-specific belief systems that prevent the realisation of that common humanity. Communicate at all costs, and if what you have to say about yourself cannot be said, then sacrifice it for the good of the human community. It is in vehement response to this strategy for the destruction of life's secret that Terror, Baudrillard argues, finds its own peculiar force in the secretion of a threat which circulates without speaking its name, without asking for any recognition, and without making a political demand. This is not simply a doctrine of 'radical otherness', it is a secretion of the truth that life *is* radically other. And until the world proves us otherwise by subordinating itself to the omnipresence of the 'hegemony of the Good' which biopolitical accounts of human being seek to achieve, we have no good reason, he believes, to think differently. It is in this context of the subversion of the regime of truth which this biopolitical war without end is attempting to secure that Baudrillard, if not as such arguing for, urges us to share in, his secret understanding of Terror.

Circulatory life: 9/11 as architectural catastrophe and the hypermodernity of Terror

THE OVERRIDING response to the event of 9/11 has been to contextualise the attack and the conflict which has ensued in apocalyptic terms. Liberal regimes are variably portrayed as engaged in a war for the defence of common humanity and for the salvation of modernity. The last chapter challenged this widely shared view of the War on Terror by reconceiving it as a war waged in extermination of the fundamental conditions for life against a form of Terror attempting to save life from its biopolitical subjugation to an increasingly global liberal apparatus of discipline and control. Yes, the future of humanity is at stake in this war, but any resolution of the conflict will only arise once we learn to question the limits of existing understandings of what constitutes life and its potentialities. Conceiving life as both that which is targeted by this apparatus as well as that which attempts to subvert liberal regimes' strategies of subjugation forces us in turn to rethink our understanding of relations between liberal modernity and the forces that we are told seek its destruction. Even within many of the critical responses to the 9/11 attack on the World Trade Center which formally inaugurated the War on Terror we find the attack itself portrayed as an act of violence visited upon liberal modernity from 'the outside' of liberal modernity as, for example, Mary Kaldor has described it (Kaldor 2003: 142–60). The alternative account of the war that we have advanced so far is based on an understanding of it as an attempt of life to escape its confinement *within* the constraints of liberal conceptions of humanity and modernity. If anything this war represents not a 'return of the outside' as Kaldor argues, but a yearning *for* an outside. The life subject to liberal modernity is here seen wrestling with itself, attempting to escape the suffocating limits which liberal regimes have secured for it.

In this chapter I want to pursue this debate further and in a contrasting way by challenging existing explanations of the actual event of the 9/11 attack itself. The attack on the World Trade Center on 11 September 2001, has been most commonly interpreted as an act of terrorism designed purposively for the mass slaughter of innocent civilians. Attempts to think about the objectives and motives involved in the attack in more complex terms are berated by liberal critics such as Jean Bethke Elshtain for 'aim[ing] to draw our attention away from the desperate office workers plunging like birds with broken wings to their deaths, trying to escape a more horrible death by fire or from buildings imploding and shattering thousands of human beings into minute bits of rubble and dust' (2003: 10). The purposive targeting of civilian life is indeed a central component of the definition of terrorism itself. As Martin Shaw argues, 'terrorism is a highly degenerate form of war, incipiently genocidal because it attacks civilian social groups in a more or less indiscriminate manner' (2003: 142).

There can be little doubt that the global impact of the attack on the World Trade Center depended not least on the fact that so many people died as a result. Never in the entire history of the United States has such a large number of civilians been killed in one single attack on American soil, and the attackers obviously knew that many people would die if they attacked the World Trade Center at such a time of day. And yet the human lives lost in the attack do not explain the full significance and impact of the attack. In fact, understanding the full significance of the event of 9/11 requires that we do precisely what Elshtain forbids us to, and think about the objectives and motives of the attack in broader terms than the destruction of human life. In this chapter, in particular, I want to think about the significance of the targeting of the buildings of the World Trade Center itself. Why these particular buildings? What was their significance? Why was the destruction of the World Trade Center meaningful? The symbolic importance of the World Trade Center, and its roles in motivating the attack, is necessarily marginalised by accounts such as Elshtain's which seek to screen out any and every way of construing it other than as the product of a fanatical desire for the destruction of human life.

In other less liberal responses one can occasionally discover the targeting of the World Trade Center explained in more symbolic terms. The World Trade Center was targeted, it is argued, for its value as a symbol of the economic power of the United States and the neo-liberal model of capitalism more generally associated with liberal regimes and societies (Harvey 2002: 58). In the now hauntingly ironic words of its architect Minoru Yamasaki, the World Trade Center was built to be a symbol of 'the relationship between world trade and world peace' (Wigley 2002a: 84). Seen in this light, the Terror attack on the World Trade Center can be understood as a political act aimed not only at causing mass civilian death but at doing so in a way that inflicted collateral damage on the American as well as a more ambiguously liberal identity. Yet as preferable to Elshtain's simplistic reduction of it as such accounts may be, they remain nevertheless superficial. There exist other more powerful ways to contextualise the symbolic value of the attack by Terror on the World Trade

Center, ways with importance for our understanding of the relation of this war to the developing crisis of liberal modernity and the role of liberal regimes in perpetrating the conditions for their own catastrophe. It is a fact that the building itself had long since been an object of hatred among New Yorkers themselves, before the occasion of its violent destruction. 'Brutal and overbearing ... expressions of an urbanism that disdained the city and its people,' described Marshall Berman (2002: 6). 'A manifestation of terrorism ... a destructive act – specifically an attack planned by the city's oligarchs and carried out with the general consent of its populace,' said Eric Darton (2002: 91–94). Within architectural theory especially, the World Trade Center symbolised not simply the economic power of the United States nor simply the overstretch of the neo-liberal model of capitalism but a much more politically complex bias toward orthogonal and especially vertical forms in the creation of city spaces within the modern era. And this privileging of the vertical and the orthogonal had found its culmination, it was argued, in the iconoclasm of the skyscraper tower. The World Trade Center epitomised that bias.

In this chapter I am going to develop an account of the significance of the 9/11 attack understood in explicitly architectural terms. To do so I will focus on the critique of the bias toward orthogonal and vertical forms in architecture developed by Paul Virilio. Virilio's work on architecture and the politics of city spaces developed in close association with that of each of the other thinkers who have so far been addressed in this book. His intellectual debt to Foucault has been well detailed (Douglas 1996), although that debt is disputed on grounds which we can consider subsequently (Redhead 2004: 38–9). His affiliation with Deleuze's co-author Felix Guattari went as far as their co-founding of a free radio station called Radio Tomate in 1979. And the comparability of many of his ideas with those of Baudrillard has been likewise an object of much discussion (Redhead 2004: 119–26; Gane 2000: 78–84; Kellner 2000: 114–15; Genosko 1994: 124–5). Virilio's critique of the function of orthogonal and vertical architectural forms is based on the same argument as that which we have developed to ground our Foucauldian analysis of the War on Terror thus far. That is to say he argues that such forms of architecture have functioned historically in conjunction with other biopolitical techniques deployed by liberal regimes in order to organise their societies logistically and strategically. In doing so, they, similar to other biopolitical techniques for the control of the life of liberal societies, do a form of violence to the life of those who inhabit them. Such forms of architecture are improper, he argues, to life. The increasing tendency toward the construction of vertically and orthogonally organised city spaces during the development of the modern era gave symbolic representation to the liberal humanist ideal, reinforced, he argues, by the gradual development of Darwinian evolutionist thinking, of mankind's superiority over its inferior animal other (Virilio 1997: 8). The erection of these architectural forms is based, he argues, upon a violent misconception of what life is and its capacity to become other than it is. That is to say its propensity for movement and change. Symbolically such architectural forms recover and celebrate an image of the life of a being 'rising up on its feet, upright ... a standing human, sometimes with his legs spread ... a profoundly static being' (1997: 8), a being which towers and commands over all that which it surveys, but never becomes or changes; a being which disavows the capacity for movement in order to achieve a sedentary stasis. And in their habitation such buildings function to reduce the life of their occupants to a 'fatality of vertical enclosure' which denies their essential nomadic capacity for movement and circulation.

From his very earliest writings on these themes, Virilio identified this privileging of orthogonal and vertical forms specifically with the design of the city of New York, so much so that he described New York itself as representative of a tendency toward the 'Babelization of the city' (Virilio and Lotringer 2002: 60). And this Babelisation of the city of New York was represented most forcefully for Virilio in the creation of the twin towers of the World Trade Center. This was a sentiment which before the 9/11 attack was shared and expressed by others. Baudrillard, in conversation with the French architect Jean Nouvel, described before the attack how

> The World Trade Center expresses the spirit of New York City in its most radical form: verticality. The towers are like two perforated strips. They are the city itself and, at the same time, the vehicle by means of which the city as a historical and symbolic form has been liquidated – repetition, cloning. The twin towers are clones of each other. It's the end of the city. (Baudrillard and Nouvel 2002: 38)

What is distinctive to Virilio's work on these problems of architecture, and the reason for making his work the focus of this chapter, is the sustained nature of his attempt to challenge and subvert the implications of orthogonal and vertical forms for the ways we inhabit city spaces. It was in resistance to this radical verticality that Virilio and others allied with him committed in the 1960s to the principle of systematically opposing the 'aberration' of the towers (Virilio and Lotringer 2002: 34). Out of this commitment was born a new architectural avant-garde that has since pursued another, nonorthogonal, antivertical vision for the city. In doing so, it declared 'a state of war' upon these 'aberrant' architectural forms (Parent 1997: ix). The argument that I will make in this chapter, then, is that to interpret the destruction of the World Trade Center in 2001 in architectural terms is to challenge prevailing understandings of its significance and symbolic value. An attack which liberal critics such as Elshtain argue to have been perpetrated by individuals incapable of humanity becomes recontextualised as an attack upon a building which symbolised the artificiality and violence of the liberal ideal of human life. Yet this artificiality was disclosed to us not for the first time in the violence of the Terror attack of 9/11. Authors such as Virilio have been arguing it to be the case for many years, and his interventions in debates on architecture have acted to make us think more critically about the ways our experience of life and our relations with others are conditioned by such peculiar spatial forms. To recognise the ways in which the 9/11 attack resonated with Virilio's architectural critique and his attempt to wage war on such forms means that the attack itself can no longer adequately be understood as an attack that came from the 'outside' of liberal regimes and societies. Examining Virilio's work is to recognise a long and substantial tradition of opposition to these architectural forms within the domain of liberal societies themselves, a loathing and political hatred for everything such buildings symbolised and the ways they condition our capacity to live. In turn we can only grasp the complex relationship of the destruction of the World Trade Center to the development of liberal modernity if we address the ways in which the attack constituted itself in alliance with such forces of resistance to liberal regimes and their techniques of discipline and control. Rather than thinking of the event of 9/11 as the first act in a new era of a war between liberal regimes and their outside, we can better think of it as a culminating act in an older war against these architectural techniques of liberal regimes for the control of the life of their populations.

War, architecture, and liberal modernity

The implications of the argument to be made in this chapter are crucial for how we understand the relations of liberal societies and the development of liberal modernity to this catastrophic event. It is quite wrong to construe Terror, as Chris Brown has also argued in a different vein (2002), as a force that emerged from outside the orbit of liberal societies, as a force without relation or responsibility to the development of liberal modernity, or as a primordial force that is essentially 'antimodern', to use Francis Fukuyama's indictment (2002: 32). Prevailing and influential conceptions such as Fukuyama's are dangerous and misleading. They are dangerous in that they ignore the many respects in which Terror is derivative organisationally, logistically, and ideologically upon ideas and practices produced within the orbit of liberal societies. They are also misleading insofar as they draw a veil over the contiguities and resonance of the attack with this already well established rejection of the basic tenets of modernity which emerged and gathered force within liberal societies themselves during recent decades. Liberal societies have, of course, as was discussed in the previous chapter, undergone profound changes in recent decades, changes which in turn have challenged their most modernist underpinnings. Since at least the 1960s, the vertically and hierarchically ordered societies of the more traditionally modern period of liberal development have given way to the emergence of more circulatory, fluid, and interactive societies. This shift has been initiated not simply by an antipathy toward a more traditional conception of modernity as elicited in Virilio's critique, but as discussed in the last chapter, by the development of new and more refined strategies for social control. Understood in this light, the attack upon the World Trade Center represents a culminating point in the overhaul of a form of modernity that was already outmoded by changes in the organisation of liberal societies in recent years. Ultimately, the argument that follows from this contextualisation is that we can understand Terror not as a force born from outside the orbit of liberal modernity but, in opposition to that reading, as very much a product of the development of liberal modernity. The weight of symbolic value that Terror derived from its attack on the World Trade Center was a product of the extent to which the vertical and orthogonal form of those particular buildings had become incongruous with the newfound fluidity and horizontality of more contemporary liberal societies. In turn, of course, such a reading forces us to rethink our understanding of the radicalism of Terror. If the function of Terror is to fulfil processes already set in train by the development of liberal modernity then how radical is it actually? This is a question, which responded to through Virilio's architectural critique, will allow us to construe the significance of Terror in terms very different to those claimed by Baudrillard in the last chapter.

To make this critique of the radicalism of Terror is likewise to pose questions of the radicalism of Virilio's own critique of architectural traditions. Virilio's critique of the orthogonal and vertical bias in the development of modern architectural forms has been made on specific grounds. As I detail subsequently, Virilio argues that the orthogonality and verticality of modern architectural forms is a product of the fact that the city bears an embedded relationship with the practice of war. The verticality and orthogonality of prevailing architectural forms derive from a historical and structural demand of the city for logistical efficiency. In complying with the demands of the city for increasing orthogonality and verticality, architecture has to assume, Virilio argued, a certain degree of responsibility. The 'war' that Virilio mobilised against the orthogonal and the vertical comprises a counter-strategy mobilised against this embedded relationship between cities and war, a war that Gilles Deleuze and Felix Guattari have otherwise described in echo of Virilio as a war waged in pursuit of 'nomos-space' against the militarised forces of striation that invest 'city-space' (1999: 481). In turn, Virilio attempted to introduce criteria and characteristics into architectural design that he claims the logistical demands of the city otherwise denies: characteristics of mobility, circulation, and fluidity especially. In contrast to claims that he attempts to reduce politics to questions of aesthetics (Leach 2000: 82–3), Virilio's work can only be made sense of as an attempt to politicise aesthetic forms. Yet Virilio's account of war and its relationship to the orthogonal and vertical construction of city spaces and its consequent denial of mobility today looks increasingly outdated. Recent years have witnessed a profound shift in the ways in which liberal regimes wage war, and the demands they make of their societies in preparing for war. The new practices of war that have emerged as a result of what is known as the 'revolution in military affairs' (RMA) exemplify and demand the very characteristics that Virilio and others located in antagonism to the logistical interests of the city: mobility, fluidity, and circulation. A question to be posed in this context, therefore, is whether or not the political framework within which Virilio contested the embedded relationship between the city and war has not itself been outmoded by the transformation in the practice of war entailed in the RMA. A similar critique can indeed be made of Deleuze and Guattari's account of the distinction between state and nomadic forms of war that in turn informed their account of the counter-strategic war through which they pursue their ideal of nomadic life (1999: 351–423). In fact, as I detail, Virilio does to some extent anticipate this critique, and the later development of his theorisation of relations between war, power, and movement leads him to turn his back on his early forays in architecture. Indeed, although the Terror attack on the World Trade Center resonates with the architectural manifestos of Virilio from the 1960s, his theorisation of relations between war, movement, power, and technology ultimately can also be used to critique the form of resistance assumed by Terror on grounds of its 'hypermodernism'.

From Architecture Principe to transurbanism: waging war on the city

Virilio's opposition to the dominance of orthogonal and vertical forms in architecture can be traced back to the period between 1963 and 1968 when, in collaboration with the architect Claude Parent, he founded the movement known as Architecture Principe. Architecture Principe declared its opposition to the dominance of orthogonal and vertical forms on the basis of an explicit claim that these forms of architecture derive from the historically embedded relationship of cities to the practice of the preparation for war. The principle of verticality in architecture derives, they argued for instance, directly from the interests of city powers in maintaining surveillance over their societies. In this context, Virilio argues the skyscraper tower to be a direct descendent of the watchtower (Virilio 1997: 7–8). The orthogonal bias in the design of buildings derives from the will of cities to render their societies docile and their movements controllable (Virilio 1997: 8). And in this context there is a close relationship between Virilio's critique of the function of architecture as a method of spatial control and Foucault's account of disciplinary spaces such as barracks, prisons, and asylums. In *Discipline and Punish* Foucault demonstrated how architecture served a function at the origins of the development of disciplinary societies in rendering space functional. Architecture played a key role in the development of the disciplinary techniques examined in the first chapter, particularly those of enclosure and partitioning. Such techniques aimed at organising space in a manner that would confine bodies in order to 'eliminate the effects of imprecise distributions, the uncontrolled disappearance of individuals, their diffuse circulation, their unusable and dangerous coagulation; it was a tactic of anti-desertion, anti-vagabondage, anti-concentration' (Foucault 1991: 143). In turn, as already discussed earlier, Foucault identified the development of these disciplinary techniques with an inversion of relations between war and society to the point where social order becomes a continuation of needs and demands originating from the order of war. That thesis has clear parallels with Virilio's argument on the relations between cities and war, and in fact Virilio went so far as to accuse Foucault of effectively stealing his thesis on the relations between architecture, discipline, and war in order to write *Discipline and Punish* (Armitage 2000: 42). What can be said, at least, is that the clear affinity between Foucault and Virilio on the nature of the relations between architectural design, discipline, and war denies the curiously under-researched claims of critics such as Steve Redhead who argue there to be no significant parallels between the work of Foucault and Virilio (Redhead 2004: 38). On the other hand, authors such as Ian Douglas who claim Virilio to be no more than a 'faithful disciple' of Foucault overstate their case too (Douglas 1996). Virilio's work on the relations between city spaces and war, and the implications of those relations for architectural practice clearly predate and preconfigure Foucault's interest in the problem of space and its relation to disciplinary practices. Foucault's later works have played a powerful role in the development of a critical human geography concerned with the function of 'institutional and settlement spaces in the management of difficult or "other" human populations' (Philo 2000: 206), but Virilio's work did from its inception in the 1960s provide a direct and pragmatic opposition to the architectural forms that enable such control of bodies and populations.

The maintenance of control and surveillance of the movements and dispositions of populations was crucial, historically, to the ability of cities to prepare for the event of war (Virilio and Lotringer 1997). In order to make its own society fit for the event of war with other rival regimes, the city had first of all to shape and condition its own population (Virilio 1986) – to remove the life of the population of all those dispositions and tendencies construed as not amenable to the conduct of war; all those elements of life not conducive to calculation and which might disrupt the aptitude of society as a whole for logistical conformity and effectiveness in time of war. In this sense, cities, for Virilio, have always been at war not only with one another but with their own populations as well. Ever since the work of Vitruvius, the original Roman author of the first extant treatise on the subject of architecture, the work of architects has been shaped, he argues, by the military, security, and strategic demands of the cities they serve. What was distinct to Architecture Principe was the fantasy, not without its antecedents (Wigley 2002b: 119), of an architecture capable of being a rival military force to the city, doing battle against the city rather than for it. Since the time of Architecture Principe, other movements within the domain of architectural theory have reoriented their ambitions to the ends of destroying the traditional roles that architecture performs in aiding the surveillance and control mechanisms of cities. This fantasy, some argue, has taken increasingly concrete form in the development of new architectural avant-gardes since the decline of Architecture Principe in the late 1960s. New movements such as transurbanism, represented by the work of Dutch architects such as Lars Spuybroek and Rem Koolhas in particular, invoke design strategies that attempt to problematise the traditional relationships between architecture, power, and war in ways that reclaim urban space for non-logistical purposes (V2_Publishing 2002).

In challenging the logistical orientation of traditional city spaces and architectural forms, this architectural avant-garde has been particularly concerned with promoting the mobility of populations as well as the mobility of the form in which city spaces are conceived. The attempt to insert a principle of mobility into architectural design can be traced much further back, at least as far as the 1832 declaration of Père Prosper Enfantin, leader of the Saint-Simonists, that 'architecture as a theory of construction is an incomplete art: the notion of mobility, of movement, is lacking in it' (Jormakka 2002: 5). Nineteenth-century architects such as Patrick Geddes pursued this idea by attempting to imagine and model the city as if it were a living organism (Welter 2002). Yet, Architecture Principe revitalised the urgency with which this commitment has been pursued on the understanding that the absence of mobility is a deficiency that derives directly from the intimacy of relations between cities and war. In doing so, Architecture Principe forged designs for buildings that, in contrast to the docility and fixity imbued in populations by traditional design, would set bodies in motion. Traditionally architecture always tends to aim at economising the movement of populations (e.g. through the incorporation of elevators and escalators) in order to increase, Virilio argues, their logistical efficiency. Vitruvius, for example, argued that the thickness of the walls of a city should be calculated 'such that armed men meeting on top of it may pass one another without interference' (Vitruvius 1960: 22). In contrast, Architecture Principe aimed to create spaces in which bodies would move and circulate freely, a built environment in which movement would be permanent and incalculable. This they pursued specifically through the elaboration of what they called 'the oblique function' (Virilio and Parent 1997: iii–v). In the creation of a building such as the Saint-Bernadette-du-Banlay chapel in Nevers, France, during the 1960s, itself a kind of demilitarised bunker, Architecture Principe created a nonorthogonal space in which surfaces are curved, inclined, or slanted; a space in which there are no horizontal floors or vertical walls; a space, instead, of permanent instability in which bodies that inhabit it enjoy no obvious resting place, have no choice but to enter into mobility. In such a space, it becomes literally impossible to stay still, instigating the actuality of the kind of radical nomadism that Deleuze and Guattari argue imbues life in the most essential ways. In such conditions as those achieved by Virilio and Parent in the construction of the chapel at Nevers, the entire dwelling becomes a mobile landscape which contrasts with the disciplinary spaces of traditional architectural forms, and thus the life of the body, they argue, escapes the state of docility through which disciplinary powers seek to control it (Virilio and Parent 1997b: vi–viii).

Contemporary and influential architects working today, such as Lars Spuybroek, have continued this commitment to the promotion of mobility in the advance of their more recent projects. In opposition to the fixity with which city spaces and their buildings have traditionally been conceptualised, Spuybroek envisages cities as systems in possession of all the properties of living organisms – soft, mobile, and transformative systems that entail the capacity to draw differentiations internally rather than just externally, to absorb and exchange information with their surrounding environments rather than defend against them, to be able to shift between states of order and chaos, to undergo fluid alterations in their structures, and to possess direction rather than form. As Spuybroek declares:

> We must opt for an architecture which stimulates life's suppleness, that enables, even encourages the subtle flow of events. Only a form which has mastered the body's motor system, is capable of activating. Only a form which has been transformed and affected by the rhythm of life, is capable of motivating. It can only prompt the body into motion as a motor, as a vector, as a combination of power and direction. (Quoted in Jormakka 2002: 74)

9/11 as architectural catastrophe

How can we use this tradition of architectural war on orthogonal and vertical forms as a means to make greater sense of the 9/11 attack on the World Trade Center? Are they completely unrelated? Is it, even, immoral, as Elshtain argues, to do so? Attempts even to broach the question of the relationship between war and architecture in such terms within International Relations itself are very scarce. A rare exception is to be found in the work of Martin Coward on the destruction of the urban environment of Bosnia during the war of 1992–1995 (Coward 2004; Coward 2002). Coward critiques the 'anthropentricism' of liberal analyses of the war which insist on the reduction of the destruction of the urban fabric of Bosnia to a 'phenomenon contingent to, and thus dependent upon, the violence perpetrated against the people of Bosnia' (Coward 2004: 158). Instead he argues that we have to locate the destruction of the urban fabric of Bosnia in correlation with the destruction of human life within a broader conflict in which it is the 'agonistic heterogeneity' of urban life that is imperilled by forces aimed at the destruction of the conditions of possibility for the expression of urbanity. The city, for Coward, is the privileged site of the expression of urbanity. As such any war waged against it is a war waged upon the condition of heterogeneity and difference without which life cannot express its urbanity.

Coward's analysis is a powerful corrective to forms of analysis which decry any attempt to shift the focus of analysis of war away from the destruction of human life as such (Shaw 2004: 148). Yet, his conception of the city as a necessary site for the expression of difference and heterogeneity is itself to be contested. What can we say of the city of New York, or of other cities within the liberal orbit? Are they, by definition, symbols of a society which privileges the conditions of possibility for the expression of difference and heterogeneity? What does such an analysis and conception of the relations between cities and war enable us to say in consideration of the destruction of, for example, the World Trade Center? Coward's own analysis, given its investment in and essentialised defence of a humanist conception of urban space as a site for the expression of life as difference, cannot provide us with tools with which to make sense of the attack on the World Trade Center as anything other than a fascistic attack upon the conditions for the expression of life's heterogeneity, as opposed to an attack waged against a building which symbolised the global subjugation of life to a biopolitical order which attempts to command difference and heterogeneity as being argued here.

In actual fact, Virilio himself has largely sought to put distance between the attack carried out by Terror on the twin towers of the World Trade Center and his own self-styled war waged upon the 'aberration' of the towers. Indeed, Virilio (2002: 81–2) himself joined in declaring the attack as the first in a new era of war rather than, as I am arguing here, the culminating point in an older one in which his own work plays a constitutive role (quoted in Redhead 2004: 3). Nevertheless, the resonance of the attack with the sentiments expressed by Virilio and other theorists of architecture is striking. In fact the decision to target the World Trade Center by its attackers was made with explicit consideration of its architectural significance. Mohammed Atta, the leader of the group of hijackers who commanded one of the planes which brought the Towers down, was himself an architect by training with a loathing for the destructions which such architectural forms had wrought upon the urban fabric of his own place of birth, Egypt (Wigley 2002a: 90). Atta is said to have viewed such forms as alien to Islamic culture (Ruthven 2004: 8). Indeed the importance of the architectural dimensions of the attack, and the recognition of those dimensions by the attackers themselves, was made explicit by Osama bin Laden himself in a speech transmitted shortly after the attack on the Al Jazeera television channel in which he made the following remark:

There is America hit by God, in one of its softest spots. Its greatest buildings were destroyed, thank God for that. There is America, full of fear from its north to its south, from its west to its east. Thank God for that ... To America, I say only a few words to it and its people. I swear by God, who has elevated the skies without pillars, neither America nor the people who live in it will dream of security before we live it in Palestine, and not before all the infidel armies leave the land of Muhammad, peace be upon him. (bin Laden 2001)

Bin Laden's suggestive reference to an attack launched by God, 'who has elevated the skies without pillars', is remarkably close in sentiment to Virilio's call for the mobilisation of a war against the imposition of vertical forms in pursuit of the recovery of 'nomos-space'. More than thirty years earlier, Virilio himself had declared that 'its demise pronounced, New York can die – we have seen worse. Nevertheless we salute in New York the final vertical city, the culmination of the second urban order. After the horizontal order of our old towns, the vertical order in Manhattan is going out' (Virilio 1997b: VI).

The point here is not to argue that Virilio was somehow directly implicated in the attack on the World Trade Center. Yet it is important that we recognise these resonances between this architectural critique of the impositions of the 'vertical order', a critique which emerged and developed within liberal societies themselves, and the motivations of those who carried out the attack on the World Trade Center. Both Virilio and those who committed the attack on the World Trade Center can be seen to have shared a loathing for what this building symbolised in biopolitical terms. Each abhorred the narrowness of the account of life, its potentialities and its exclusivities, authorised in such architectural forms. For Virilio, the World Trade Center encapsulated an idea of a form of human life which is artificial, imperial and violent. The Twin Towers celebrated the humanist conceit of a life which stands erect and still, which can be quantified and qualified, given a definitive form replete with boundaries which in turn allow the distinction to be drawn between that which human life is and that which human life is not. A form of humanity, which, upon account of the recognition of its boundaries and its towering distance from those other forms of life against which it defines itself, issues its imperial command to which it demands obedience. The abhorrence of those who committed the attack on the Twin Towers emerged from the experience of being the body identified with those other forms of life which the biopolitical body defines itself against; the body which is towered over, objectified as belonging to a culture and a form of society which is deemed able only to struggle to achieve the heights of humanity, and the relation with which must be cultivated in order to create the correct conditions for which development toward a more perfected human form might flourish; the experience in turn of being a body which has no means to legitimise its own understanding of life outside of the boundaries already drawn for it by those who claim access to the laws of humanity.

Yet, while Virilio and those who destroyed the World Trade Center can be said to share an abhorrence for the account of life encapsulated in that particular architectural form, it becomes more difficult to reconcile them in terms of the ways in which they respond to the question of what life might otherwise be and what life may become once freed from the constraints of a liberal humanist account of what life is and what life may become. In opposing the sovereign fixity of the liberal humanist account of life, Virilio invests all his faith in the alternative ideal of a life which, somewhat akin to Deleuze and Guattari's account of nomadic life, refuses fixity, desiring only the conditions of its own becoming. The vertical and orthogonal order of the city exists only as an obstacle to the possibility of being able to remake the city in pursuit of 'the meta-stability of a human mobility which is indeed proper to life' (1997: 9). Yet this investment in a concept of life as that which yearns to become other than it is, which knows only restlessness and movement, is not easy to reconcile with the account of life idealised by Terror. The defiant life of Terror, aiming as it would appear to be, at the restitution of a mystical order grounded in an insistence upon life's subordination to transcendental law, is if anything starkly opposed to Virilio's conception of life's immanent desire for mobility.

Indeed we could go further than this to argue that Virilio's critique of vertical order and the architectural forms which symbolise a society based on the principles he identifies as antithetical to life, has itself already been outmoded in the development of architecture since the 1960s: outmoded, even more importantly, by a shift toward a form of society and regime of power relations which more closely approximates to his own account of what life is in terms of its restless desire for movement. In the previous chapter I examined Baudrillard's account of the contemporary transformation of societies consequent upon the shift in liberal strategies of control toward more circulatory forms – to the extent that I argued, with reference to Baudrillard, that Terror itself is understandable as a distinct mode of subversion of a form of political regime which functions by seizing life's most immanent tendencies for movement in order to generate a form of society based precisely on a principle of circulation. In the context of liberal regimes within which the biopolitical command of life requires the perpetual circulation and interaction of different life forms, Baudrillard depicts the radical resistance of a form of Terror which refuses power's insistence upon movement and interactivity. Indeed Baudrillard's own forays into debates over architecture have involved an attack on buildings such as the Beaubourg in Paris which, as he describes it, epitomises an ideology of circulation, movement, and interaction (1994). In the context of a globalised regime in which the ability to circulate, to move, and interact with others are necessary for the reproduction of political order, Virilio's advance of an architecture designed to foster the capacity for movement, circulation and change looks somewhat dated. In turn it becomes more difficult to reconcile his ideal of an architecture that will create city spaces in ways more amenable to life's immanent desire for mobility, and the architectonics of Terror based as they are on the counter-ideal of a life which refuses the demand for circulation and movement upon principle.

The avant-gardism which Virilio advanced in the 1960s, and which in turn has engendered its own cult of anti-orthogonal work within architecture since, is now fairly reconcilable with the discourses and ideologies of advanced liberal societies based as they are on principles of the right to movement and circulation. The shift within architecture from the traditional stress on verticality and orthogonality toward circulation and movement is, in this sense, only part of a broader social and political transformation that liberal societies have undergone in recent decades. Indeed this architectural shift can only be made sense of in the context of the shift in liberal strategies which Baudrillard describes, and which we addressed in the previous chapter, from societies ordered by hierarchy and fixed antagonisms to orders in which circulation is the rule. The rigidity of the traditional structures of modern social organisation, premised on essentialised forms of identity, particularly nation and class, has given way, he argued, to new fluid forms in which societies are coded according to principles of differentiation rather than antagonism, circulation rather than opposition (Baudrillard, 1999b: 92–4). The upshot, according to many of the ideologues of this form of society, is the realisation of a greater freedom of communication, greater liberty in the definition of social identity, and more flexibility in the movements of peoples territorially as well as socially (Castells 1996). With the compression of space and time identified with the globalisation of liberal societies, mobility especially has become the chief signifier of freedom (Marchand, Reid and Berents 1998: 974–81). The circulatory characteristics of liberal societies today are celebrated for the greater facilitation of communication, liberty, and movement they are said to offer. The form of critique offered by Architecture Principe of the orthogonal and vertical bias of traditional architectural forms has, it can then be said, already been absorbed in the transformation of liberal societies in recent decades. This is obvious in the domain of architecture, in which the dominance of and bias toward orthogonal forms has gradually been eroded and displaced by a new penchant for the development of dynamic, fluid, nonorthogonal forms. Architectural forms are increasingly geared toward the promotion of mobility and the maintenance of fluidity of structure. The World Trade Center, that celebration of the orthogonal and the vertical, became, it can be argued, in the period of its own lifetime, an increasingly outdated representation of the main values of liberal societies. The targeting by Terror of the World Trade Center appears in this light not so much an attack upon a major icon of liberal modernity but rather an attack upon an already decaying monument to a form of society that has itself already been eroded and displaced by new more problematic forms.

This argument gathers yet more force when we look at the reconstruction of the space previously occupied by the World Trade Center for the purpose of memorialisation. Daniel Liebeskind, the architect awarded the contract for the redesign of the space as a memorial, was himself significantly influenced by Virilio, contributing to the republication of the manifesto of Architecture Principe in the 1990s (Liebeskind 1997: 157–9). Liebeskind's plan for the reconstruction of the site is designed, as Michael Shapiro has described, precisely to avoid 'narrative closure' (Shapiro 2004). Visitors to the memorial, a sunken pit in the place where the Towers once stood, will be provided with no guidance as to how to use, interact with, or interpret the space, being left to find their own way of passage through it. In fact the space itself has been redesigned, at least at proposal stage, to avoid any sense of a definitive boundary between the space of memorial and the space that lies beyond. 'The memorial park's western boundary, the so-called slurry wall that held back the Hudson River from flooding in after the 9/11 attack, will continue to restrain the river … there will be … no firm demarcation of what was and what became. Where the wall was, it still is, and in such a place memory is a live event. History plays out in real time' (Liebeskind, quoted in Shapiro 2004).

Shapiro makes a strong case for construing Liebeskind's design as a counter-hegemonic response to America's sense of itself pre-9/11, yet we need to be more careful in thinking about the significance of these new archetypes of architectural form which Liebeskind's work captures so acutely. Virilio himself, while laying the foundations for the development of the new anti-orthogonal and anti-vertical forms which are increasingly reshaping the practice of architecture in liberal societies, has ultimately sought to distance himself from the manifestos of Architecture Principe and its utopian understandings of the potential for a boundless and oblique architecture of mobility. If we track the development of Virilio's ideas on relations between war, architecture, and cities after the decline of Architecture Principe in 1968, we find a very different theorisation of the relations between the city, movement and war, a theorisation that leads Virilio to reject the dimensions that underlay the arguments made by Architecture Principe for the waging of war in the name of movement up until 1968. In turn, examining his account of the role of movement in the reproduction of what we can call the 'circulatory city' allows us to proffer a different perspective on the significance of Terror's attack on the World Trade Center, a building which figures less as an iconoclastic representation of the new regimes of power that govern the circulatory city as a symbol of an already outmoded social form.

War, movement, and the circulatory city

Virilio's preoccupation with architecture only lasted up until around the period of 1968, when following the uprisings and revolts which rocked Paris that year, his relationship with his collaborator on the project, Claude Parent, quickly fell apart (Redhead 2004: 27–31). Parent shared none of Virilio's enthusiasm for the political potentials of the movements that emerged in 1968, especially their revolutionary ambitions and claims. Virilio, on the other hand, found much to identify with in movements such as the Situationists and their own attempts to wage war in retrieval of the city. Yet Virilio's own work after the dissolution of Architecture Principe, and after the relative failures of the movements of 1968 to realise their revolutionary ambitions became apparent, developed a fundamentally reconceived account of the relations between cities, movement, and circulation. The main principle of the organisation of city spaces is, he argued, henceforth, not simply the preparation for war with other regimes beyond, but the mobilisation of a form of permanent war of movement within the city itself. We are as populations, he argues, constantly being mobilised in a war of movement against the city itself. This principle of achieving organisation by cultivating a relation with war in the order of the city has, he argues, explicit historical origins. It originates from the efforts by which early cities would cultivate the territories which surrounded them through the construction of protected enclaves and enclosures in advance of attacks by nomadic enemies. By doing so, cities were able to anticipate the movement and regulate the speed of advancing attacks by nomadic societies. This device of cities evolves over time, he argues, to become *the* principle upon which the city learns not only how to control the movements of its own populations in logistical preparation for the event of war with other rival regimes, but how to shape the movements of the enemy too – the art of strategy. Operating through the dissemination of 'strategic information', the city learned, he argues, to pre-emptively shape and condition the movements of the nomadic enemy beyond (Virilio 1990: 17).

The development of this strategic device leads over time, Virilio argues, to an inevitable blurring of the boundaries between the city and the space of its enemy. Shaping the space of the enemy pre-emptively, conditioning its tendencies and movements to a degree that gradually erodes the boundary between the city and its outlying areas, meant that eventually the distinction between the logistical function of the city as a space for the preparation for war and the strategic space where the city closes with its enemy becomes outmoded. In its place what is created is a zone of indistinction in which the practices of logistics and strategy gradually coincide. At some point in the eighteenth century, Virilio argues in his *Speed and Politics*, this process of development reached a point of fruition. From this period onwards, the principle concern of governing regimes is not with the logistical preparation of the population for the event of war with an external other, but with the control of the population within as the site in which enmity arises. The strategic relation with the enemy beyond the city becomes transformed into a relation with the enemy which resides in the propensity of the population to resist order within. Yet at the same time this emergence of a new form of security dilemma and war-relation within the city creates a new motor of development which the organisation of the city itself feeds on – to the point where Virilio is even able to quote the Nazi Joseph Goebbels to the effect that 'the ideal militant is the political combatant in the Brown Army as a movement ... obeying a law that he sometimes doesn't even know, but that he could recite in his sleep ... Thus we have set these fanatical beings *in motion*' (1986: 4). The power of the city construed in this way is no longer a power which controls movement in the name of preparation for war, but which relies upon it, as a means through which to seek an ever increasingly fluid and circulatory form of organisation. The organisation of the city rests fundamentally, he argues, in texts of the 1970s on an unrecognised order of political circulation, in the street (1986: 4). Spatial organisation within cities, population distribution, the regulation of movement, and the creation of signal systems by which to economise speed within cities all, according to Virilio, were recognised explicitly as being central to the strategy by which the city suborns its society as a political end in itself rather than a merely logistical means in advance of strategic engagement.

The tendency of cities toward ever increasingly diffuse forms of movement, more complex orders of circulation, culminates, he argues, in a hypermodern order in which mobility and circulation is the rule. And yet it is precisely these rules which are being employed in the design strategies of the architectural avant-gardes which have sought to follow in the wake of Virilio's Architecture Principe. The design strategies of transurbanism especially, its solicitation of a shift in the conception of the form of order that a city may entail, one from simplicity to complexity, stability to chaos, stasis to movement, is derived heavily from the cybernetic and complexity sciences which Virilio argues to be complicit in the development of this circulatory order. Architects such as Rafael Lozano-Hemmer (2002), for example, have introduced the concept of relational architecture, based on an adaptation of ideas from cyberneticists Humberto Maturana and Francisco Varela's (1980) theory of autopoiesis. Lars Spuybroek (2002) derives ideas from the biophilosophical discourse of complexity to reconceive the 'soft city'. Arjen Mulder (2002) argues that is necessary to remodel the city in the 'self-organizational' terms of neo-Darwinian theories of evolution, which Virilio himself had explicitly polemicised against in his tracts of the 1960s.

In turn, we have to ask whether this cybernetic discourse, with its emphasis upon movement, instability, and fluidity, is really suited to the ends to which it is being put – that of the destruction of the embedded relations between war and the city – or whether in fact the development of this avant-garde, and the new architectural forms pursued by it, is not in fact creating the archetypally biopolitical city in which life lived as perpetual movement is itself a game of strategy. In turn we can argue that what we are seeing emerge in the development of so-called transurban architectural forms, and the redevelopment of city spaces consequent upon such ideas, is the emergence of a new regime of relations between war and the city. An avant-garde that claims for itself the capacity to challenge the age-old relation of architecture to strategy and logistics is in fact, we may as well say, remaking that very relation.

How, then, should we understand the relation of Terror to this newly emergent social and political as well as architectural form within liberal societies? If we consider the logistical organisation of the groups such as Al Qaeda identified with Terror, we can see that they exhibit many of the features that are celebrated of contemporary forms of liberal societies. Al Qaeda is often described in terms of the fluidity of its networked organisational form, ultimately drawing comparison with the organisational structures of the most advanced forms of business corporations (Gearson 2002: 17). Logistically and strategically, the force of its threat is said to be born out of its transnational character, its capacity to organise globally and to target populations regardless of location and habitat. It is said to make full use of global media networks, both to facilitate communication for itself between cells and to maximise the political impact of its attacks. While it is commonly portrayed as operating upon an ideology of the total rejection of liberal modernity, in organisational structure and strategy, it is extremely consistent with the contemporary characteristics of the most liberal of societies. Even the religious basis of its supposed ideology could be said to be consistent with the broad revitalisation of spiritual beliefs that is commonly identified with the hypermodernisation of liberal societies in recent year (Castells 1997: 12–27).

But it is in terms of its tactical deployment of weaponry invested by the very forms of technology and scientific knowledge with which liberal societies have consistently proclaimed and celebrated their advantages over other rival forms that Terror's contiguity with liberal modernity becomes most perspicuous. The attack on the World Trade Center was defined ultimately by the redirection and acceleration of forms of technology on which the ordinary functioning of liberal societies are fully dependent. In these senses, Terror fulfilled the description that Virilio and Lotringer made shortly before the attack on the World Trade Center of a new form of warfare called 'the total accident' (2002: 153–61). Every form of society, Virilio and Lotringer tell us, is conditioned powerfully by the technologies that it relies upon. And every form of technology provokes a type of accident that is particular to the utilitarian dimensions of that society. The role of Terror, it would seem from Virilio's perspective, has been to instigate the total accident of the hypermodern circulatory city – at the very least, to pursue what Virilio and Lotringer also identify in terms of the accident as the continuation of politics by other means, and in doing so to direct advanced technologies of speed and motion, coordinated via diffuse flows of information through various information networks, at one of the most fixed, visible, but also and crucially *decadent* symbols of liberal modernity (2002: 154). Ultimately, if we are true to Virilio, we must understand the constitution of the attack in terms of its expression of a hypermodernity, a product of already existing and prevailing technological, social, and political forms that liberal regimes themselves have nurtured and developed.

Doing so, therefore, provides us with a very different conception of the life of Terror to that which we developed in the previous chapter through Baudrillard. Baudrillard argued that we can understand Terror as a form of defiant life which succeeds in standing outside of the development of liberal modernity and the strategies of biopolitical regimes for the striation of life. Terror as defiant life, is understood as such as attempting to recover the irreducible mystery and obscurity of life against the advance of biopolitical regimes of power dedicated to the destruction of that mystery and terror by offering a form of subversion which such regimes are incapable of comprehending. In this sense Baudrillard believes the Terror attack on the World Trade Center to have been a 'pure event' which destroys the stagnating development of liberal societies in recent years (Baudrillard 2003: 149). In contrast, interpreting Terror through the optic derived from Virilio as we have done here, allows us to challenge this claim as to the subversive logic of Terror. The emergence of Terror is understood simply as the fulfilment of a set of conditions and dynamics brought into play through the excessive development of liberal societies predicated upon principles of circulation and movement. Terror exhibits a form not of defiant life, but of circulatory life that has gone out of control. It prospers, it is said, from the excess of circulation which accrues to a radically globalised world.

It is in fact precisely this embodiment of Terror within dynamics that are basically consistent with the hypermodernisation of liberal societies, that has led many of the more conservative of critics within the United States to argue that it is necessary to respond by retrenching a form of international order which will undercut the global networks of circulation upon which Terror, it is believed, is reliant. As Audrey Kurth Cronin argued in chapter 3, 'international terrorism is not dangerous because it can defeat us in a war, but because it can potentially destroy the domestic contract of the state by further undermining its ability to protect its citizens from attack' (Cronin 2002). Virilio's response to the phenomenon is less nostalgic. There can be, he argues, no slowing down of the pace of development of this 'machine' he identifies with the development of liberal modernity and its biopolitical regimes of power. The major mistake that liberal regimes have made, in the development of their increasingly refined systems of circulation and their ever increasing exercise of power over life, is to believe that the 'speed of the machine is in the service of humanity' (Virilio and Lotringer 2002: 153). It is in opposition to the naïvety of liberal humanist accounts of the development of information and communication technologies and their life invasive sciences that Virilio posits his belief in the necessity and inescapability of the accident. The accident of 9/11 was the accident of a world over-conditioned by the biopolitical insistence on movement and circulation. Yet, contrary to Baudrillard's more salvatory reading, Virilio identifies in the actuality of this accident no possibility of the retrieval of a world or an account of life with any redemptive potential. His conception of the accident of 9/11 is utterly apocalyptical. This accident is to liberal societies and their regimes what sin is or was to what once was known as 'human nature' (Virilio and Lotringer 1997: 182). The strategisation of life within biopolitical regimes, its subjection to their techniques of manipulation, has reached, he believes, an extreme limit, in the context of which these systems have no alternative other than to implode.

The theological dimensions of Virilio's thought lead us a long way from the political questions and issues of the forms of agency and intervention that we might think ourselves capable of enacting in response to these dilemmas, and which underwrote the accounts of the War on Terror and the problems it poses for how we might think and pursue life differently in earlier chapters. Virilio, similar to Baudrillard it would seem, leaves us little space or energy for a conception of agency or for a political response to the advance of liberal modernity and its machinic subjection of life to biopolitical law. Everything and nothing is at stake in the differences between the accounts of Terror developed by these two strikingly similar but starkly opposed thinkers: Terror understood as a defiance which salvages life from the conditions of its subjection, versus Terror understood as a circulation which implodes its conditions for expression.

Yet lest we think that the development of Foucauldian thought on this problem leads necessarily to the rejection of politics, and the rejection of any capacity for struggle and engagement with the problem of biopolitics and the limitations it places on our capacities to respond to the question of what life is and may become, we turn in the next chapter to a radically different conception of the potentialities of life after liberal modernity and its culminating War on Terror, that of Michael Hardt and Antonio Negri. For Hardt and Negri the era of Terror remains an era of immense political challenges and possibilities: the challenge of generating new forms of political resistance to global liberal regimes, and the possibility of establishing new ways of collectivising human agency in excess of the logistical parameters established by liberal regimes. It is to their more optimistic response to the event of 9/11 that we now turn.

Biopolitical life: the 'war against war' of the multitude

LIBERAL societies, while founded upon the challenge of the mastery of war in the name of a commitment to the promotion of peace and the enabling of human life, appear today to have rendered their subjection to the condition of war all but intractable. The mere sustenance of liberal societies now requires their permanent mobilisation for the waging of a war without end against an enemy of Terror which threatens the existence of the logistical way of life identified with the development of liberal modernity. Terror can be understood as threatening liberal societies with an excessive fulfilment of the logistical imperative, as was argued in the previous chapter. Or it can be understood, as was argued in chapter 4, as operating upon an outright refusal of the logistical value of life on which liberal understandings of the 'quality of life' depend. And yet, in attempting to mount a defence against the force of this threat, liberal societies have, as was argued in the second chapter, never been as staunch and transparent in their commitments to the possibilities of sustaining logistics as a way of living as they are currently. In this context of intractability, failure, and *hubris*, it befalls us to search for another response to this problem. Another response, which given the biopolitical stakes of this conflict, must in turn mean a different response to the question of what life is and what life might become when it does not succumb to the logistical account of life on which the security of liberal societies is claimed to depend. Indeed, it was precisely the possibility of such a response which we already began to pursue in the third chapter by developing a thought as to the forms of nomadic life which by their definition seek to escape the constraints of logistical ways of living.

This final chapter pursues this problem of what life is and what life may become outside of its capture within the forms of logistical order promoted in the name of a War on Terror, through recourse to the work of two of the most currently influential of all Foucauldian thinkers, Michael Hardt and Antonio Negri. What defines the work of Hardt and Negri, and certainly what has helped make their work so popular in recent years, is their attempt to reconstitute the historical tradition of refusal of and resistance to the logistical ordering of liberal societies. Negri's work especially, has from its inception been dedicated to the aim of liberating the 'value of life' from out its subjection to the logistical strategies aimed at it. Throughout liberal societies there rages, he has argued consistently, a 'permanent civil war' over the political constitution of life (2003: 124). In making this claim both Negri and Hardt have attracted much attention for their attempts to forge an alliance between a Foucauldian understanding of the 'biopolitical contexts' in which global liberal regimes of power control the life of their societies (Hardt and Negri 2001: 23–7) with a Marxist understanding of the biohistory of liberal power relations as embedded in processes of capitalist expansion (2001: 221–4), and a Deleuzean conception of the nomadic refusal that life offers to biopolitical regimes of control (2001: 212–14). Critics of their work have tended either to berate them for their abandonment of what are perceived to be traditional premises of Marxism (Boron 2005: 105–6; Wood 2005: 6; Callinicos 2002: 319–22), or to embrace them for their innovative redeployment of Foucauldian, and more especially Deleuzean motifs (Alliez 2004; Holland 1999: 108; Massumi 1999: 201–4).

Yet to date there has been no substantial attempt to grapple with their underlying theory of the relations between war, liberal regimes and the governance of life, although this is sure to change given that their most recent text, *Multitude* (2004) has made this the central problem at the heart of its exposition. For Hardt and Negri there can be no explanation of the ways in which societies and subjectivities have struggled to escape the biopolitical shackles with which liberal regimes have bound them without addressing the paradoxical function of war in both the organisation of liberal societies and in the development of resistance to liberal regimes' logistical strategies. As such, Hardt and Negri's work is defined by the development of an account of the biopolitical contexts of both the wars waged by liberal regimes upon their populations as well as of the wars of resistance to liberal regimes that those subject to them have developed in conjunction. It is precisely this paradox of war as the practice which conjoins the development of the biopower of liberal regimes alongside the development of the biopolitical life of what they call 'the multitude' which resists its regimentation that has become the major focus of their work.

In this respect the resonance of Hardt and Negri's conception of the problem of war and its relations to liberal societies with those of Foucault, as well as Deleuze and Guattari, is very strong. Hardt and Negri attempt to develop an account of the influence of war upon social organisation which echoes Foucault's major claims, attested to in chapter 2, as to the function of war as the source of a disciplinary schema which has been gradually applied to societies as a whole and which aims at the total control of life forms and processes. In turn, however, they are attempting to reconcile such an account of war's function as a source of subjection with a more Deleuzean stress on the necessary failures of such a totalising project. In echo of Deleuze and Guattari, Hardt and Negri argue that life, given its essential nomadism, necessarily escapes the attempts of any regime to apply the war-schema to it. There is an irreducible capacity of the multitude to escape the attempts of regimes to govern it. In turn this irreducible capacity of escape comes down to the superior ways in which the multitude itself wages war in contrast with the logistical strategies of the regimes concerned with governing it. Indeed Hardt and Negri's latest work *Multitude* revolves around an attempt to clarify this distinction between the 'war of the multitude' and the wars conducted upon it by liberal regimes. In this text they pursue the question of whether it is

> possible today to imagine a new process of legitimation that does not rely on the sovereignty of the people but is based instead in the biopolitical produc-tivity of the Multitude? Can new organizational forms of resistance and revolt finally satisfy the desire for democracy implicit in the entire modern geneal-ogy of struggles? Is there an immanent mechanism that does not appeal to any transcendent authority that is capable of legitimating the use of force in the multitude's struggle to create a new society based on democracy, equality, and freedom? Does it even make sense to talk about a war of the multitude? (2004: 80)

Yet in spite of the resonance of this problem with the debates on relations between war, life, and liberal societies in the works of their forebears, Hardt and Negri ultimately struggle to do justice to either Foucault or Deleuze and Guattari. As we will see in this chapter, the ways in which they theorise the distinctions between the wars of the multitude and the liberal way of war are fundamentally problematic. In particular, their development of a concept of 'democratic violence' grounded in the 'biopolitical productivity' of the multi-tude is especially questionable. Through this concept they attempt to establish grounds for the legitimisation of a form of war qualitatively different to both the biopolitical techniques of legitimisation on which the current wars of liberal regimes depend while avoiding what the authors believe to be the trappings of Terror as a method of resistance to the imposition of the liberal way of war. In stark contrast with Baudrillard's account of Terror as defiant life, Hardt and Negri argue that Terror is futile in that it is providing the very conditions of legitimisation upon which the current expansion of liberal regimes globally through war is now occurring. Terror, currently, they argue, is

> allow[ing] those in control to consolidate their power, claiming the need to unite under their power in the name of humanity and life itself. The fact is that a weapon adequate to the project of the multitude cannot bear either a symmetrical or an asymmetrical relation to the weapons of power. To do so is both counterproductive and suicidal. (2004: 346)

In contrast to the 'horrible practice' of Terror (2004: 45), Hardt and Negri attempt to account for a concept and practice of 'democratic violence' grounded in 'biopolitical production' as a way of conceiving how life contests its subjection to the logistical strategies of liberal regimes. Democratic violence is, all the while, a form of what they describe as 'war against war' (2004: 342). In a manner that echoes Deleuze and Guattari's attempts to qualify the wars of nomadic societies in terms of the defiance of the powers of sovereignty by attempting to refuse rather than fulfill the ideal of sovereignty (Deleuze and Guattari 1999: 420–2), they qualify democratic violence as a way of making war without adhering to the same techniques employed by liberal regimes, nor diametrically opposing them in the 'horrible' manner which they argue to be the case of Terror (Hardt and Negri 2004: 342).

Their claim as to the ways in which the democratic violence of the multitude succeeds in distinguishing itself from both liberal war and Terror will be subject to critique here on expressly Foucauldian grounds. Especially important is Hardt and Negri's attempt to legitimise the democratic violence of the multitude on grounds of its supposedly defensive character. The 'democratic violence' of the multitude is different from the pre-emptive and 'creative' violence of liberal regimes (2004: 341), they state, because it attempts only to 'defend society, not create it ... democratic violence does not initiate the revolutionary process but rather comes only at the end, when the political and social transformation has already taken place, to defend its accomplishments' (2004: 344). Yet, as I will argue, such a conception of the legitimacy of violence in terms of its defensive qualities is intrinsic to the very liberal tradition of war which they are attempting to stand outside of. Indeed, it is this very qualification of war as a defensive means toward the promotion of human life which Foucault's later works, most especially his lecture series *Society Must Be Defended*, attempts to expose as the source of the problem of war's intractability in the era of liberal modernity. Hardt and Negri perform a very similar manoeuvre when they attempt to qualify 'democratic violence' as a defence of the 'biopolitical productivity' of the multitude. Given Foucault's own critique of the martial propensities of biopolitically qualified forms of life, this is an especially peculiar concept for two Foucauldians to deploy in resolution of the problem of war. Indeed, ultimately, their account of the biopolitical life of the multitude is vulnerable to precisely the same criticisms of the limitations of the liberal way of life that we have developed in previous chapters.

Not only is it difficult to reconcile Hardt and Negri's attempt to legitimise a form of war against Foucault's critique of the biopolitical techniques which have underwritten liberal regimes throughout modernity, but the outline of a theory of the democratic violence of the multitude also struggles to do justice to Deleuze and Guattari's original conception of nomadic war from which the authors claim much inspiration. Hardt and Negri's account of democratic violence is based upon a claim that war has become an increasingly immanent power of societies, and that this rendering immanent of war is the product of a historical process of struggle through which the multitude has gradually undermined the abilities of regimes to govern it. Yet this is at best a simplistic reduction of Deleuze and Guattari's account of the relations of liberal modernity to the phenomenon of war wherein the development of liberal regimes is explicable on account, Deleuze and Guattari argue, and as was discussed in the third chapter, of the immanent investment of the function of war as a tool for the organisation of liberal societies. By this they mean that while previously war existed as an instrument of intervention which regimes exerted from above upon the populations they sought to govern, today war plays an immanent function within liberal societies in the production of forms of subjectivity that are increasingly self-governing. The function of war, as such, is brought immanently within the ordering practices of liberal societies rather than being applied from above or outside. In this sense, also, Hardt and Negri's theory of democratic violence celebrates narrative developments which from a more authentically Deleuzean perspective are deeply complicit with the increasing strategisation of liberal power relations in and among societies.

The rest of this chapter proceeds as follows. The next section provides an account of the development of the theory of the war of the multitude as it occurs in Negri's political thought. We can then examine how this contributes to the more recent account of Hardt and Negri's conceptualisation of the 'two wars of liberal modernity' through which, as they argue, the antagonistic relationship between the multitude and liberal regimes has developed. Then, in the final section we can address the problem of how this antagonism has been complicated by the emergence of Terror as a resistance to liberal regimes, and the question of whether Hardt and Negri are able to usefully distinguish their account of the contemporary character of the war of the multitude from it.

Negri's account of polemical being

Negri's political thought has been dedicated toward, from its inception, a certain valorisation of war. For Negri this valorisation owes much to the ways in which he has sought to build, from early on, upon the neglected legacies of Benedict de Spinoza's political philosophy. From 1979 until 1980 Negri found himself, as a result of his involvement with the militant group known as the Red Brigades in Italy, imprisoned awaiting trial on charges in connection to the kidnapping and murder of the politician Aldo Moro. During this time in jail he wrote copiously, producing a substantial work on Spinoza, published subsequently as *The Savage Anomaly*. It was in this seminal work that Negri most thoroughly developed his now widely celebrated concept of 'the multitude'. While critics of his work today often operate on the false assumption that this concept simply describes a new form of social movement concerned with resistance to the contemporary formation of liberal regimes (Boron 2005: 18–19), it actually originates in Negri's work more authentically as a philosophical account of the 'human condition' (1991: 188). Through a close reading of Spinoza, Negri develops a philosophical account of the 'absolute immanence', passions and emotion, desire and volatility, love and affective relationality, that he argues distinguishes human life. The social and political development of humanity has depended on and can indeed be explained on account of, Negri argues, the increasing empowerment of these immanent tendencies of humanity throughout modernity. Whether such an ontological account of the human is vindicated in Hardt and Negri's subsequent accounts of democratic violence is something we will want to consider later. However, at its origins in Negri's work, this account of the absolute immanence of human life, which he identifies with Spinoza's political philosophy, is most crucially important for the ways it differs from liberal accounts of humanity which found their explanations of the political and social development of the species in what they argue to be the necessary subjection of human life to transcendental forms of law. Premodern social orders were, of course, very obviously organised through the subjection of human life to the transcendental laws of religious codes. In the modern era, on the other hand, political and social theory has been dominated by figures who have argued for the rejection of religiously ordained truths while valorising new forms of transcendental power and meaning. In the work of major liberal political philosophers and theorists such as Kant, or more recently John Rawls, this renewal of transcendental law occurs, although applied differently, in their insistence upon the subjection of the immanent potentialities of human life to a 'schema' of reason (Rawls 1980; Kant 1964: 471–81). Negri, in contrast, invests in Spinoza's rival belief in the immanent potentials of human being, its rational desires to explore the outer limits of its powers of transformation and creativity over and against the insistences of liberal theorists on the subjection of such desires to architectonic schemas and systems.

The argument for the subjection of human capacities to transcendental schemas of reason by liberals has consistently been made on grounds, as we know, of the demand for peace. Without the subjection to the schema of reason as Kant claimed, society descends into a state of barbarism, of Hobbesian war of all against all. Yet the forms of architectonic order achieved by liberal regimes do not, as we already know, remove the problem of war from society. If anything the development of liberal modernity testifies only to the perennial if changing character of the problem of war within and among liberal societies. It is in the context of this failure that Negri finds considerable explanatory purchase in the alternative tradition of thought of Spinoza concerning peace and war. Through Spinoza, Negri develops concepts of the horizon and temporality of war. These concepts of a horizon and temporality of war emerging out of Spinoza define, for Negri, likewise a radically anti-liberal tradition within the canon of Western political thought (1991: 112). The legacy of Spinoza *contra* liberal political philosophy, for Negri, is the conception of the necessity of a horizon and temporality of war to forms of political subjectivity as opposed to the utopian ideal of a time and space of peace. Against the fundamental argument as to the necessary surrender of the subject's 'right of making warre' to political sovereignty (Hobbes 1985: 234), Spinoza's work allows Negri to develop the concept of the 'polemical being' of 'the multitude' whose temporality is war and the life of which is fought for at the 'horizon of war' (1991: 118). Subject to the imposition of the modern 'zero time of peace' the multitude is compelled for Negri to retrieve and create anew the 'time of life' through war (Negri 2003: 123).

From the Spinozist position developed by Negri in his early work, any attempt to impose peace from above or outside through force and law, or any more insidious attempt to manipulate the dispositions of the subjects that make up a society in order to render them more amenable to peace, is doomed to fail. As he expresses it, humanity is defined fundamentally by its potent, indestructible, and versatile character (Negri 1991: 145). Wherever a form of transcendental power attempts to make a decision as to the way of life its society must lead in order to preserve peace, whenever any attempt is made to determine the boundaries, either ethical or territorial, that human life must remain within in order to preserve peace, a violent injustice to the essence of life itself is enacted. The life of human being, given its immeasurable definition, always by necessity refuses the forms and boundaries insisted upon by regimes attempting to govern it in the name of peace. The development of human subjectivity is itself, according to Negri's reading of Spinoza, an expression of continual battle, of a struggle between contrary forces and drives, desires and passions. In its essence the formation of the human subject as well as of intersubjective relations and ultimately of society is born out of as well as through this essence of war. This is not, from the Spinozist point of view, in any way a negative observation. Understanding the nature of humanity as such is, as Negri argues through Spinoza, to redefine the terms upon which we may construe the nature of human freedom, of the potentials for peace, and of the problem of war. The concept of war expresses what Negri describes as the 'constitutive dynamic of being' (1991: 147). It is what accounts for the ways in which the human subject forms and undergoes change, establishing new ways of life, new conditions of expression, new relations, and social possibilities. Freedom finds its expression in the complexities of subjectivity and social relations born out of this constitutive dynamic of war. Such a war is in this sense productive rather than negative. It produces human freedom, and such freedom can only be won by empowering and giving expression to it. The multitude is, ultimately, a definitive expression of this constitutive dynamic of war. And the greater freedom it establishes the more it can be said to be at war as the complexity of war relations are a condition for the production of its ever increasing freedom.

Given its essence in war, its dynamic and indestructibly open character, the multitude cannot by definition be governed. Every attempt to determine its form or manipulate its disposition in order to sustain peace leads it to respond with the invocation of war in order to out-manoeuvre the strategies by which governance is being applied. When the integrity of its immeasurability is called into question by any form of transcendentally inclined power, the multitude responds by invoking its condition of war as a means with which to escape such strategies of subjection. The multitude is defined by its continual movement toward a 'horizon of war' (1991: 118). The function of this concept of the horizon is not dissimilar from Deleuze and Guattari's equally Spinozist concept of the 'frontier' in *Anti-Oedipus*, to designate the limit at which the organisation of societies and subjectivities undergo processes of deterritorialisation and enter upon lines of flight (2000: 281). Likewise the horizon of war, for Negri, expresses a point of, as he describes it, 'ontological pregnancy', where the polemical being of the multitude 'presses for more, not satisfied with the horizontality that it has achieved, with its beautiful and animated flatness' (1991: 119). The horizon of war, then, in this context is fairly comparable with Deleuze and Guattari's articulation of it as that space in which forms of life are deterritorialised in the movement toward other directions and possibilities over and against the conditions of peace that are imposed upon them by transcendental forms of governance.

In the only recently translated essay 'Constitution of Time', written during the same period of imprisonment on charges of the murder of a politician, we discover Negri arguing directly for 'war' and likewise for war to be recognised as 'the reality of the relationship' between the governing and the governed (2003: 124). In turn he urges that we 'cannot speak of peace [then], but only of differentiated moments in a permanent civil war' (2003: 124). While it is tempting to read such proclamations as barely veiled validations of that political murder, they are nevertheless continuous with Negri's profound philosophical effort to reconceptualise liberal understandings of war and its embodiment in an immanent ontology of being. If Negri's *Savage Anomaly* was concerned with the multitude's spatial existence at the horizon of war then 'Constitution of Time' attempts to articulate a conception of the war of the multitude understood as a specific type of temporality. Again, this concept of a time of war owes much to Negri's reading of Spinoza. Negri locates Spinoza's concept of time in opposition to the other more traditional and dominant conceptions of the time of modernity understood as necessary and determinate historical development (Negri 2004: 83). For liberal theorists such as Kant, modernity represented the fulfilment of historical developments, the purposes of which are located in the realisation of the transcendental law of reason, and to which the contingencies of life must necessarily be suborned. Spinoza, on the other hand, provides Negri 'a theory of time torn away from purposiveness' (2004: 90); a time of 'presence', the integrity of which cannot be suborned or measured against any form of teleological standard; a time 'which is autonomous stability and rootedness against any dispersive mobility of the "they" and to any form of cultural disorientation' (2004: 85).

The two wars of liberal modernity

From this Spinozist perspective developed by Negri, then, the creation of liberal regimes, the development of mechanisms and techniques with which to govern the processes by which subjects form and societies develop, is bound to fail in so far as it misapprehends the immeasurable and indestructibly potent nature of their object of governance, the multitude. Each attempt to establish peace through transcendence invigorates the constitutive dynamic of war through which the multitude develops its increasingly complex forms of subjectivity. Yet this condition of war between transcendental forms of power and the multitude is not static, it is dynamic and interactive. As such the powers of transcendence are not only continually being foiled where their projects of peace are concerned. The forms of transcendental power to which the multitude is subject are themselves being transformed in this very process of interaction with the ever evolving and re-emerging immanent powers of the multitude. The more that the multitude demonstrates its immanent capacities for transformation to the forms of transcendental power opposed to it, the more those forms of transcendence are led to invest their methods of control immanently within human beings. Power, in this context, is forced to become increasingly biopolitical as a result of the multitude's tendency to refuse any and every attempt to impose order from above. Indeed this is precisely how Hardt and Negri go on to explain, or at least argue for, the gradual development within modernising societies from the bare reliance on a formal state apparatus to the increasingly biopolitical modes of governance of liberal regimes that define the organisation of contemporary global societies (2001: 22–41). The development of biopolitics is explicable only on account of the irreducibility of the multitude's polemical being to governance. The intensity of power's interest in and control of human life results from this perennial challenge posed at power by the polemology of life itself.

If Negri's early works provided a deeply philosophical account of what the multitude is, his three co-authored works with Michael Hardt are more directly geared to addressing contemporary political and social issues. In the context of the development of Negri's theory of the problem of war, their second co-authored text *Empire* is very important. Here Hardt and Negri advance their case in a clearly expedited fashion, that the development of modernising societies can be understood essentially not in terms of a historical movement toward an increasing peace, the conditions of which are laid out for us by the transcendental laws of reason and the regimes of governance designed to instill them, but rather as the expression of a double movement in which such regimes of governance are created retroactively in order to impose command and control over the newly discovered powers of immanence which were, they argue, by the sixteenth and seventeenth centuries, threatening the very constitution of societies, their laws, norms and established hierarchies. 'Modernity is', they argue, 'from its beginnings a war on two fronts' (2001: 77). The discovery and development of humanist forms of scientific knowledge and a new understanding of the immanent potential of life over and against its subjection to transcendent law challenges existing orders of knowledge, thrusting the sovereignty of the traditional political orders into crisis. These new forms of knowledge intersect powerfully, as Negri himself argues, with the development of the political conviction in the human perfectibility of society, expressed most forcefully in the republican tradition. This humanist republican tradition is, as Negri describes it, 'polemical when confronted with any ideology of representative government and any statist praxis of alienation' (Negri 2004: 32). In turn, these humanist republican movements become enmeshed in an internal conflict with the new regimes of governance designed to block them. The new humanist movements found the development of new forms of political thought, for which the quest for a perfectible human social order is grounded in the commitment to war as a condition of possibility for the development of political subjectivity. In turn this new form of 'polemical being' finds itself fighting a war against these regimes in order to preserve the integrity of its grounding in the ontology of war. It is necessary in order to preserve the active existence of the multitude in war to fight a reactive war against transcendental political powers insistent upon the imposition of forms of peace which violate the multitude's polemical being. It is in this doubly political and ontological context, that the multitude finds itself at war, struggling for life. It has to wage war in order to survive and propagate its newly discovered location in the space and time of war as a condition of possibility for human life.

This narrative which Hardt and Negri construct in *Empire*, where the modernisation of societies is made possible by the double entry of war and life into political order and where power is a struggle to command the polemology of life itself, owes, of course, much to Foucault's original analysis of biopower and biopolitics. The authors of *Empire* profess as much (2001: 22). Indeed there is a beguiling similarity between, on the one hand, Hardt and Negri's understanding of the development of liberal modernity animated immanently by the polemical being of the multitude, as well as riven by a war between this polemical being and transcendent forms of power intent on controlling it, and Foucault's understanding of the specificity of biopolitical regimes of power born out of an immanent investment of war and life within them (Foucault 1990: 92–100).

Yet, it pays to be a little more circumspect as to the Foucauldian dimensions of Hardt and Negri's work. Upon closer inspection, their theorisations of the relations between war, life and liberal modernity are significantly different. In Foucault's work, to recall, the development of biopolitics is a dystopian narrative through which life's entry into the domain of political order is only possible on account of its gradual submission to the logistical strategies of liberal regimes (1990: 141–2). This process of the biopoliticisation of life is possible, Foucault argues, because techniques for the preparation for and conduct of war suddenly start to become inverted and applied immanently to the organisation of life within societies (1990: 102). This combination of life's entry into political order and the immanent investment of techniques deriving from war for the organisation of life, is not in any sense, for Foucault, an emancipative event in the history of humankind. Rather, consequent upon this event, human life is, according to Foucault, made to submit to an unprecedented martial regime of discipline and subjection. The idea of a society composed as a common body, defined by an origin, a shared genesis, and an evolutionary potential, all of these attributes which the life of society accrues in the context of liberal modernity, derive from what is, Foucault argued, an essentially logistical demand for increasingly efficient forms of organisation. In turn, the production of subjectivity within such a logistical context becomes disciplined and regulated by the very same laws. The subject that is formed within biopolitical power relations is, as Foucault described, a 'strategic' subject that is continually struggling to survive, waging a war in pursuit of the possibility of the truth which she or he is, a truth that is continually being reconstituted in antagonistic relation with other equally strategised subjects. As such the whole of social relations becomes a kind of 'strategic field' in the contexts of which subjectivity is continually being reproduced, developed, and complexified. The greater the strategisation of this field the more complex and hybrid the forms of subjectivity it discloses become.

If we compare this understanding of Foucault's of the specificity of liberal power relations involving the dual entry and investment of life and war within them with that of Hardt and Negri, the differences are striking. For Foucault, the application of techniques deriving from war to the organisation of life, the implications of that application for the forms of life that societies give expression to, as well as the ways in which subjects come to be produced in such a context, are utterly contingent features of liberal modernity. All of his later works from *Discipline and Punish* onwards were about problematising this application of war to life and exposing the limitations that it places upon our understanding of the problem of what human life is and might yet become. To a certain extent, it has to be said, he failed in this project. When placing himself in the position of attempting to think life and its definitions beyond or outside the strategic model of power and the forms of subjectivity it induces he tended himself to resort to fetishising it. In the later volumes of *The History of Sexuality*, for example, this failing is expressed in the development of his concept of ascesis as a kind of counter-strategic practice by which subjects can actively intervene in the processes by which their subjectivities come to be produced by waging war upon themselves. The practice of ascesis for Foucault must take, as we saw in chapter 3, 'the form of a battle to be fought, a victory to be won in establishing a dominion of self over self' (1992: 91). The practice of intervention upon the self is itself conceived in a martial manner. Yet, there can be no doubt as to the essential if unrealised nature of his theoretical project.

In the lecture series he gave at the Collège de France during 1975–6, only recently translated under the title *Society Must Be Defended* (2003), it becomes especially clear that the main theoretical task Foucault was posing himself toward the end of his career was that of how to escape the very discourse of war as a foundation for thinking about politics. In this vein Foucault was not simply concerned with the martial origins of liberal regimes and their societies narrowly conceived, but more crucially with the martial underpinnings of the revolutionary traditions of thought and practice set up and developed nominally to contest those regimes. In *Society Must Be Defended* Foucault argues that the logic which explains the forms that war takes in and among liberal regimes is to be located in the origins of modern social struggles, even in the very republican traditions that Negri has sought to venerate (2003: 50). Of central concern in this respect is the theme of race. In *The History of Sexuality* Foucault made the claim that it is as 'managers of life and survival, of bodies and the race' that liberal regimes have been able to wage wars biopolitically (1990: 137). In *Society Must Be Defended* we find Foucault incorporating these propensities of liberal regimes, their biopolitical foundations, involving their racialised ideologies of inclusion/exclusion, within a genealogy that involves the origins of modern social struggles. As he argued it was in the development of revolutionary social movements that the modern discourse of race first appeared (2003: 59–60). Indeed, it is only as a result, he argues, of the historical inversion of revolutionary discourses of race, where political struggle is understood as a continuation of a war with a rival race, that liberal regimes have been able to wage war, specify enemies, and create modes of inclusion/exclusion on the racialised grounds that they have. Modern regimes of governance, he continues, colonised this originally revolutionary discourse of 'race war' and inverted it to their own ends. In turn it becomes a 'discourse of a battle that has to be waged not between races, but by a race that is portrayed as the one true race, the race that holds power and is entitled to define the norm, and against those who deviate from that norm, against those who pose a threat to the biological heritage' (2003: 61). Foucault's most powerful argument throughout *Society Must Be Defended* is that if we want to understand the biopolitical character of liberal war, the tendencies of liberal regimes to construe dangers in biological terms, and to wage war on enemies that are characterised variously as animals and vermin, then we have to examine

[*113*]

the complex genealogical relations between revolutionary strategies aimed at seizing power and governmental strategies dedicated to its defence. For it is in the former, he argues, that we find the thematic of 'race war' first appearing.

If we contrast that position of Foucault's with Negri's the differences are striking. In Negri's work we find a more or less open embrace of the discourse of war as a foundation for the resistance of the multitude to regimes attempting to govern it. When in his early works Negri describes, through a reading of Spinoza, the horizon and temporality of war, he lapses into eulogy. In contrast to Foucault's severely dystopian portrait of the implications of war's investment within modern power relations, Negri paints a vastly optimistic picture. The war he depicts between the immanent forces of the multitude and the transcendental powers of regimes attempting to govern it bears witness, if we accept his account of it, only to the ontological superiority of immanence over transcendence and the gradual delegitimisation of liberal violence. Modernity is the story, for Negri, of the gradual overcoming of liberal violence through the persistent struggle of immanence for its expression over and against any and every transcendental law.

Wars of the multitude

In spite of these gulfs separating Negri's theoretical celebration of the 'polemical being' that animates 'the multitude' and Foucault's biopolitical critique of the polemological origins and dimensions of revolutionary political thought, Negri proclaims to draw inspiration and influence directly from Foucault's account of the problem of war. (Negri with Dufourmantelle 2004: 68–9). His most recent works with Michael Hardt, *Empire* and *Multitude*, both involve attempts to draw on Foucault as well as Deleuze and Guattari to theorise the current status of the wars of resistance that traverse power relations globally. Published just after the 1999 protests against the World Trade Organization in Seattle, *Empire* has become increasingly identified with the new forms that wars of resistance are said to be taking in the global era. In turn, Hardt and Negri are adamant as to the importance of the contemporary moment in the development of the multitude's wars against global liberal regimes.

This importance is grounded, they claim, in the new forms of organisation that social movements have developed in recent years. Historically, movements dedicated toward political resistance and revolt have been defined by a strong sense of collectivity. Indeed it has traditionally been argued that this is one of the major prerequisites of successful organisation for political resistance. 'An historical act can only be performed by "collective man", and this presupposes the attainment of a "cultural-social" unity through which a multiplicity of dispersed wills with heterogeneous aims, are welded together with a single aim, on the basis of an equal and common conception of the world' (Gramsci quoted in Laclau and Mouffe 1985: 67–8). Yet, as Hardt and Negri argue, such collectivity is necessarily attained at a cost. Revolutionary and resistant forms of social collectivity have historically been as defined by tendencies toward exclusivity as the regimes which they have been organised to contest. In attaining power, collectivities whose original concern was the contest of forms of violent exclusion and oppression, have tended to exhibit the very same forms of violence. War has remained the condition of their political possibility in ways that have merely led to the replication of the problems of war, violence and insecurity rather than being able to overcome them. Indeed, as indicated in the previous section, this was precisely the foundation of Foucault's critique of revolutionary traditions of thought concerned with achieving power through the means of war.

In response to this Foucauldian critique, Hardt and Negri's account of the multitude in *Empire* as well as in their subsequent text *Multitude* describes the ideal of forms of social collectivity which manifest a strong sense of commonality while encouraging and indeed pursuing the proliferation of differences and singularities. Recognising the tendencies inherent within any collective project to generate violent forms of exclusivity, Hardt and Negri argue that the multitude must radicalise the function of war in its constitution as a common body, generating differences and new forms of singularity, as a means to fend off the processes of ossification through which boundaries form and defensive violence ensues. Indeed it is this very commitment to the generative power of war as a condition for the attainment of new degrees of diversity and difference, new ways of life, which defines their concept of the commonality of the multitude. It is because it recognises the tendencies of social bodies toward wars of violent exclusion in defense of particular ways of life that the multitude must wage war upon itself, as it were, in order to overcome that propensity of collectivities toward ossification.

In turn, it is now argued in some areas of International Relations that the new forms of movements emerging to contest power in the twenty-first century do a measure of justice to this more open and reflexive way of conceiving collectivity. For example, Stephen Gill, while arguing in a more neo-Gramscian vein, has described the new multiplicity and diversity of the forms of social movement that emerged at Seattle as 'expressing new potential and forms of political agency' (2000: 137). Optimists such as Gill proclaim these new forms of social movements that emerged at Seattle and beyond as representing a new era of antagonism with the global liberal order. And for Hardt and Negri, the diversity and multiplicity of these movements can be understood as an outcome of the constitutive role of war in generating singularities and differences within the movements themselves. Hardt and Negri argue that these movements are both effectively at war with the global liberal order as well as developing in accordance with the fidelity to the principle of war which Spinoza's original and ontological account of humanity was based upon. It is this latter fidelity to the ideal of the horizon and temporality of war that accounts for their increasingly horizontal organisational forms and the complexities of political subjectivities to which they give expression. The social movements of the twenty-first century are becoming in their actuality, Hardt and Negri claim, multitudinous. And for these reasons they claim that the current conjuncture of global politics is a repli-cation of the form of conjuncture that defined the European world of the seventeenth century.

There can be little doubt as to the somewhat exaggerated nature of the claims Hardt and Negri make as to the character of political struggle at the current conjuncture. Indeed a slew of critics have lined up subsequently to tell them so (Barkawi and Laffey 2002; Callinicos 2002; Shaw 2002; Walker 2002). At the same time one has to admire the audacity as well as integrity of their attempt to push the limits of our potential to overcome this problem of war and its relation to liberal modernity. This degree of audacity, the scope with which they conceive and lay out for us the nature of the problem of war and its relations to issues of power, collectivity, and exclusivity, expresses no doubt a certain form of debt to Foucault. They do at least exhibit the signs of having read him and identified the importance of the problem of war to him. Yet in appraising their attempts to overcome this problem we have to look very carefully at their response. Indeed, it is only in the context of a basic misconception of relations between war, life, and liberal modernity that Hardt and Negri are able to make the forms of argument and claims as to the potential of the multitude to over-come the problem of war that they do. In turn it is possible to critique their conceptualisation of the multitude from a more authentically Foucauldian posi-tion.

Critiquing *Multitude* biopolitically

In terms of their broad theorisations of the relations between life and war we have already seen the significant differences between Negri and Foucault. For Foucault the investment of war within modern power relations gives rise to the techniques by which life comes to be seized, shaped and manipulated by liberal regimes. It gives rise to the dystopia of a modernity in which life is constantly being strategised by power, striated into forms which are not natural to it but contingent to the interests and demands of the pacifying regimes that life is subject to. It also gives rise to the biopoliticisation of life through which the boundary of division between life that may live and life that may die is drawn and upon which war against life is declared. For Negri, on the other hand, the immanent investment of war within power relations is the source for all that is creative and positive about modernity. It is through exploring the immanent investment of war within power that modern societies have been historically able to develop an increasingly complex array of political subjectivities, and by which they have gradually been enabled to overcome the very problem of sovereign violence. This investment of war within modern political orders is realising, as far as Hardt and Negri are concerned, increasingly horizontal forms of society in which laws, rules and norms are bent to fit the desires and needs of a multitude to which the principle of law, norm and rule is ontologically offensive and politically to be contested. In turn it is increasingly divesting societies and subjectivities of their violent differences, enabling them to converge, create and conjugate new forms of life within and between which war remains the motor of their development.

The full nature of this disagreement becomes yet more perspicuous in terms of their startlingly different employments of the concepts of biopower and biopolitics. For Foucault the concept of biopower is used 'to designate *what* brought life and its mechanisms into the realm of explicit calculations and made knowledge-power an agent of transformation of human life' (1990: 143). The concept of biopower, for Foucault, signifies not only the novelty of the subordination and amenability of human life to power within the context of modern societies, but moreover, a form of agency at work in creating that novelty. Biopower signifies not only the event of the entry of life into power but *that* which 'brought' life into the realm of power. The concept of biopolitics, in turn, signifies merely the techniques by which biopower is exercised 'in its many forms and modes of application' within societies (1990: 141). Biopolitical techniques, within the Foucauldian framework, designate the ways through which biopower is continually being reproduced and how, in turn, the subordination and transformation of life consequent upon the advent of biopower's reign is guaranteed and sustained.

For Hardt and Negri on the other hand, the nature of biopower as well as the relationship between biopower and biopolitics is very different. In the first instance, while using and developing Foucault's concept of biopower, they are concerned to take him to task for what they argue to be the ambiguity of the form of agency which that concept designates within his work. As they declare in *Empire,* if 'we were to ask Foucault who or what drives the system, or rather, who is the "bios," his response would be ineffable, or nothing at all. What Foucault fails to grasp finally are the real dynamics of production in biopolitical society' (2001: 28). In wanting to overcome this ambiguity they attempt to separate out the concepts of biopower and biopolitics from one another. In Hardt and Negri's work therefore, while biopower refers to the ways in which life comes to be seized and subject to the needs and demands of power, biopolitics refers in contrast to the contestation of such seizure and subjection by life itself. Indeed, Hardt and Negri go beyond the mere separation of these concepts, to argue that the biopolitical aspirations of life actually precede the development of the forms of biopower by which life is seized and manipulated. Modernity is not defined in the terms that Foucault offers us as the dystopian event of the subjection of life to a newly emergent regime of biopower, but by the essentially revolutionary discovery of life's immanent productivity, what Spinoza defined for Negri as its potency, versatility, and indestructible resistance to stasis. The revolutionary power of what they account for as 'biopolitical production' is likewise possible because of the immanent investment of war within life which contrasts so markedly with Foucault's understanding of the strategisation of life which occurs consequent upon war's investment into modern power relations. The forms which life assumes amidst the imposition of biopower are always, from the position Hardt and Negri advance, merely residual effects of the revolutionary advances being made by life biopolitically. Life itself is the main operator in Hardt and Negri's account of political modernity in a way that contrasts markedly with Foucault's arguments as to the ways in which modern societies are founded upon the denial of life's rooted tendencies.

In *Multitude,* Hardt and Negri draw upon a long genealogy of social struggles in order to substantiate their claim as to the agency of 'the bios'. From the German peasant wars of the sixteenth century through the peasant revolts that ruptured the development of capitalism in Europe throughout the subsequent era, to the struggles of colonised peoples against European expansion, to the English, French, Russian, and Chinese revolutions, to the guerrilla wars of the Cold War era, to the late twentieth-century struggles against neo-liberalism, and now crucially to the struggle against war itself, Hardt and Negri identify the advance of a revolution, of the gradual realisation of a biopolitics that is defined by essentially democratic ends. As they argue, the progressive route of this development is expressed in the increasingly democratic organisation of the struggles themselves. From the centralised formations of the people's armies of early European revolutions, to the more decentralised model of guerrilla organisation, to what they proclaim to be the absolute democracy of the diffuse networks resisting the global liberal regimes of the present, Hardt and Negri identify the advance of the biopolitical productivity of the multitude. In the development of the organisational forms of these struggles what we witness, they argue, is the constitution of an increasingly endless social form, a social form which escapes boundaries and anthropological definition, in order to achieve a kind of absolute state of generation and productivity.

This more or less teleological stress on the increasingly horizontal forms which social organisation appears to be taking in the modern era, and the role of war in constituting them, owes much no doubt to that other significant influence upon them, Deleuze and Guattari. Deleuze and Guattari's analysis of the development of modern societies was based on the claim that capitalism provides the mechanisms for a radical reorganisation of power, firstly from that of preceding historical social formations, and secondly within capitalist societies themselves. The organisation of power, according to Deleuze and Guattari, has shifted from the hierarchical model of despotic and savage societies to the rhizomatic and immanently invested forms of the liberal era. In turn, in their text *A Thousand Plateaus,* Deleuze and Guattari contextualise a narrative of the effect of capitalist development upon liberal societies in tandem with an account of the role of war within it (Deleuze and Guattari 1999: 351–423). The dynamism and mobility of liberal societies is explicable on account, Deleuze and Guattari argue, of regimes having immanently invested the deterritorialising powers of war within their own social orders. By this they mean that while pre-liberal societies were subject to forms of militarised intervention from the outside which in turn would lead to their reordering, liberal societies internalise this principle in order to generate a self-perpetuating process of change and self-governance. The function of war, as such, is brought within the organisation of power within liberal societies rather than being applied from the outside. In turn, it can be argued, the internalisation of this function allows liberal societies the capacity to achieve unprecedented states of decentralised organisation. Again, in rather stark contrast with Hardt and Negri's own account however, this is not a simplistically utopian development that Deleuze and Guattari attempt to account for. The point for them was to grasp the ways in which this shift involves the incorporation of the function of war as a means with which to better refine the organisation of power's machinery. And indeed the immanent investment of war within the organisation of society does not for them preclude the problems of transcendence and sovereign violence. They argued forthrightly that it is through these developments that sovereign power becomes reconstituted and new forms of political violence legitimated. Cases of historical fascism, most especially in Nazi Germany, where the sovereign violence of the Third Reich was the more powerful for the ways in which it played upon the adoration of German society for its Führer, are used to prove their point.

It is clear that Hardt and Negri develop the concept of the multitude in order to overcome the problem of the ways in which any and every social collectivity runs the risk of turning fascistic and resorting to its own peculiar form of sovereign violence. Any collective form of life, where it settles within specific boundaries and limits, creates the battle space of a division from other forms of life existing outside those boundaries and limits. In this context, Hardt and Negri's solution is to invert the order of that relation and render war an active principle of collective life in order to fend off the formation of fascism. Indeed, in their latest text *Multitude* they present us with an account of the present conjuncture in global politics as a conflict between precisely these two tendencies: on the one hand, the movement of liberal regimes toward a permanent state of exception in which war is reduced to a policing function to prevent the emergence of forms of life inimical to liberal order, and on the other the mobilisation of movements dedicated toward the contest of liberal regimes through the biopolitical promotion of life's productive potential for difference and diversity. The biopower of liberal regimes versus the biopolitical life of the multitude, as it were. In turn the multitude is forced anew into the position of having to, as they argue, 'wage war on war' by denying biopower the limits and boundaries it would impose on life and by working toward the possibility of more 'democratic' life forms. In a practical sense the text attempts to build bridges between the various forms of anti-globalisation and anti-capitalist movements which drew succour from *Empire* at the close of the twentieth century and the newer social movements within liberal societies dedicated more directly to the contest of the liberal way of war at the beginning of the twenty-first.

In attempting to forge a theoretical platform for the development of resistance to the liberal way of war today, Hardt and Negri have inevitably been forced to address the historical traditions of pacifism. In a certain sense, in developing their concept of 'war against war' what Hardt and Negri are attempting to do is steer a course somewhere between pacifism and traditions of revolutionary violence. This becomes clearer in the development of their concept of 'democratic violence'. The concept of democratic violence is not, of course, new. In a ground-breaking work published in the early 1970s the political philosopher Ted Honderich argued that political violence, where it is directed to an increase of democratic ends such as greater freedom, justice, and equality can readily be understood and legitimated as democratic (1976: 90–116). Although democracy and violence are usually construed as antithetical concepts, Honderich argues that liberal regimes which define themselves as democratic are necessarily dependent on the function of violence. Violence is systematically employed by liberal democratic regimes in order to sustain their legitimacy in manifold ways. Likewise, where political violence against liberal regimes or within any nominally democratic society or system occurs, it is possible that such violence may be understood as democratic provided it can be justified as pursuing and enabling causes of justice, freedom and equality.

Hardt and Negri pursue what is in fact a very similar argument in *Multitude*. The contemporary conjuncture of global politics is for Hardt and Negri born out of the long struggle between the desire for democracy of the multitude and the strategies of regimes which seek to govern that desire. The global liberal regimes of the present are renewing this struggle today through the imposition of what they describe as a 'constant threat of violence that effectively suspends democracy' (2004: 341). The War on Terror is, they argue, illegitimate in so far as it is aimed at actively intervening upon and destroying any form of life that does not meet its own preconceived conceptions of what does and does not constitute a danger to the logistical life of liberal societies (2004: 20–1). The endless provision of the potential for violence unleashed by the declaration of the War on Terror is the main obstacle now facing the democratic project of the multitude. It is in this context that the multitude is today forced into a position of waging what they describe as 'a war against war' (2004: 342).

In declaring the multitude's 'war against war', therefore, Hardt and Negri must distinguish it from what they understand to be the illegitimate ways of liberal war. As such, they attempt to qualify the democratic violence of the multitude in *defensive* terms. In spite of the embodiment of the multitude itself in ontological attributes of creativity, versatility, and potency, its violence, they argue, is of a purely defensive character. 'Democratic violence', they state, 'can only defend society, not create it ... democratic violence does not initiate the revolutionary process but rather comes only at the end, when the political and social transformation has already taken place, to defend its accomplishments' (2004: 344). In this sense, then, the violence wielded by the multitude, the essence of its 'war against war', is, Hardt and Negri argue, precisely the opposite of what the multitude itself is in essence. While the multitude may be defined for Hardt and Negri by its constitutive powers of transformation and versatility, it deploys violence only ever in defence of those powers. The violence of the multitude is, then, a definitively post-revolutionary form of violence. And it is definitively democratic in so far as it refuses and indeed opposes the possibility of any form of violence that might seek to threaten the democratic constitution of life itself.

All of this is fairly consistent, then, with Negri's account of the concept of war as it developed in his philosophical readings of Spinoza. Yet the contrast and resonance with the account of the problem of war and political modernity that Foucault provided in his lecture series *Society Must Be Defended*, at this point becomes very striking. There, Foucault was concerned to demonstrate the ways in which the inversion of the relation between politics and war upon which all originally revolutionary discourses are founded ends up propagating the very forms of defensive violence which Hardt and Negri are so readily committed to. As Foucault demonstrated, the biopolitical wars of liberal regimes have their origins in diverse traditions of revolutionary war. The fermentation of revolutionary wars throughout the seventeenth and eighteenth centuries eventually created revolutionary regimes which, in turn, declared their own biopolitical wars, and Hardt and Negri deploy precisely the same move in order to legitimise the right to war of the multitude. 'Democracy', they argue, 'must use violence only as an instrument to pursue political goals' (2004: 342). As such they attempt to subject the war of the multitude to the very same principles of legitimacy and strategic efficacy with which Carl von Clausewitz, the original modern philosopher of the liberal way of war, attempted at the beginning of the nineteenth century (Reid 2003b; Clausewitz 1993).

The imperia of biopolitical life

As we have seen, the attempt of *Multitude* to conceptualise a form of democratic violence, and to distinguish it from that of both traditional revolutionary violence as well as from the violence of governing regimes, is thoroughly consistent with Negri's earliest works. Yet, an as fundamental underlying ambition of *Multitude* is to conceptualise such a radical form of violent subversion in opposition to the current strategy of subversion represented by Terror. As remarked earlier, Hardt and Negri dismiss the utility of Terror as a strategy of subversion in claiming that it effectively provides the conditions for techniques of legitimisation with which liberal regimes are able to intervene and expand globally in the interests of 'humanity'. The major ambition of *Multitude* is to subvert conventional understandings of the limits of liberal understandings of human life in order to justify the subversion of liberal societies in the name of the promotion of life. Biopolitical life is, on their account, a life empowered by the exercise of war upon itself in the production of ever more complexly differentiated forms of subjectivity and society; in turn, a life which only ever resorts to violence in defence of its condition as that which Negri earlier described as 'polemical being'. Such an account of the biopolitical life of the multitude is distinct certainly from the forms of defiant life with which we earlier conceptualised the subversion of Terror through Baudrillard. Unlike Baudrillard's account of the defiant life of Terror, biopolitical life seeks subversion through the establishment of alternative forms of organisation founded upon the communication of truths (Negri 2005: 57–8). Rather than rejecting the demands for communication and interactivity embodied in the logistical strategies with which liberal regimes attempt to govern life, biopolitical life attempts to radicalise them and put them to its own use.

If anything, what is striking in the account of the biopolitical life of the multitude afforded by Hardt and Negri is its lack of distinction from the liberal account of logistical life. Subversion in the twenty-first century will reside, Negri has been arguing since the 1980s 'in the non-negotiable and irrenouncable declaration of a certain number of truths, such as: equality, freedom, opposition to selection, opposition to death, the promotion of life, the future, plans for knowledge and society ... Subversion is the radical nature of the truth. It is an applied form of this radicalism' (2005: 59). The 'promotion of life' and the holding to such other 'obvious truths, in particular the norm against killing' (2005: 59) are, Negri argues, expressions of the radicality of the subversive counter-strategies of the multitude. And yet, as we have already argued, is it not precisely in opposition to such an account of life, founded upon an organisational demand for greater and more intensive forms of knowledge about life, better communication as a way of life, subordination of life to the fear of death, and the normative prohibition to think life in any other terms, that Terror has discovered its calling? Might it not be precisely in rejection of the limits of such biopolitical imperia that Terror has developed and offered its own radically hostile account of what life is and can become?

'One can summarize in the following manner the imperatives of the immeasurable for the singularities that constitute the multitude: do not obey, that is be free; do not kill, that is generate; do not exploit, that is constitute the common. In other words, you will be able to decide the common' (Negri 2003: 258). The distance between such imperial accounts of what life is and what it may become, and the critiques opened up of the political limitations and historical specifici-ties of such accounts by the other Foucauldian authors addressed in this work is little short of startling. In this context Hardt and Negri's work fails, ultimately, not simply to do justice to the theoretical problematic of war, liberal modernity and logistical societies established by Foucault. It exacerbates the real and exist-ing political crises of liberal modernity which Foucault's work on these theoretical problems was dedicated to exposing. The question of how to liberate life from its subjection to the logistical strategies with which liberal regimes have sought to command and control it throughout the modern era remains open to inquiry and debate. And until a more meaningful and sustained intervention upon this problem is delivered, logistical life, we can presume, will continue to be haunted by the spectre of its Terror.

It is important therefore that Hardt and Negri's work does not become viewed as a panacea in the development of Foucauldian approaches to problems of war and peace, nor wider issues of international relations. If anything the rather stunning failings of their work to do justice to the problems of relations between war, life, and politics which Foucault first exposed ought to act as the instigation for a more concentrated attempt to overcome these fundamental dilemmas. The great paradox and crisis of liberal modernity that Foucault first identified remain with us. Liberal modernity is characterised by a type of society that has sought refuge from the indeterminacy of life, its radical undecidability, in techniques of discipline, regulation and normalisation, which in turn have exacerbated unprecedented and now endless forms of warfare inter-socially. The problem of modernity was never that of the problem of war as such but in the still prevalent forms of liberal solution to war. That is to say in the ways liberal regimes construe peace. Understood thus, the imperative question of politics, which Foucault also specifies, remains with us too. That is the question of how to disengage from the dual processes of subjectification by which life comes to be variably pacified and mobilised. What form does life take when it is no longer suborned to a liberal teleology of peace achieved through the means of war? Yet, in posing this question, Foucault abandoned us upon a word of prohibitive caution. Those many and long traditions of counter-opposing the imposition of peace by declaring it war, which find their culmination now in a multitude of dispersed and discontinuous offensives, provide no substantial ground, he argued, from which to escape the peace/war schemata. If we desire a resolution of this paradox of liberal modernity we must establish other ways of construing the life of political being, ones which compromise its seemingly endless polemologies.

Epilogue

The liberal desire for the removal of life from its subjection to the condition of war, and its will to secure global conditions for the peaceful flourishing of humanity, is futile. This much has long since been known. However the liberal project has not failed simply because it struggles to recognise, as other studies have amply demonstrated, the depth and complexity of the roles of war and violence in constitution of the societies and formations of political power it has sought to transform in the interests of humanity. Nor has it failed because its core principles are open to abuse as ideology by essentially illiberal political actors. Each of these lines of argument has been made and substantially explored in critiques of the necessary failures of liberalism as creed and political project in areas of International Relations to date. Instead, and as this book has sought to argue, the liberal desire to save human life from its subjection to the condition of war has failed foremost because it is itself a polemological and ultimately terrorising project which can only proceed on the basis of the most resentful violence against life. The liberal execution of the desire for humanity's salvation from the condition of war has done a continual violence to the life of humanity because it has proceeded on the understanding that it is possible to decide once and for all what that life consists of, how it might be defined, and in contrast with what other forms of life it is that human life comes to know itself as human and against which it must therefore seek to secure itself. Such a desire could never be realised or pursued other than with recourse to violence because implicit in its design is the will to sever human life from its relation to those other non-human potentialities which sustains its very capacity to know itself as a living force. In essence, by seeking to sever humanity from its relation to life through violence, liberal regimes find themselves confronted today by the irreducible vitality of that relation. That vitality is expressed in the attempts to defend the integrity of alternative problematisations of the question of what life is and what it may become under human conditions. The name given to the defence of that vitality today is Terror.

What distinguishes the body of Foucauldian thought in which this critique of the liberal project has been made here is an attention not simply to the logical inconsistencies of liberal accounts of humanity in the abstract, but to their origins and development in military institutions and practices organised for the delivery of instrumental violence against life. At the same time, the forms of life defined as human that liberal regimes have sought to promote and defend throughout modernity owe their existence not simply to the capacities of those regimes to deploy military violence against other inhuman forms of societies and subjects beyond their own territorial borders, but to the prior subjection of the life of their own societies and subjects to techniques of invasive violence through which the virtual border between what counts as human and inhuman has been historically, and is still today, maintained. There can be no restitution of the liberal desire to solve the predicament of human life's subjection to war because its own solution to that predicament was, from the beginning, dedicated only to refining that subjection, rendering human life's militarisation more insidious. When liberal regimes proclaim currently that it is 'our way of life' and 'our freedom' that they are fighting to defend they refer to forms of life and freedom which originated and developed merely as logistical resource, struggling to express themselves other than in the idiom of a social and political utility where the freedom of life was and is subject to a strategic calculus based upon demands for the increase in productive capacities, greater efficiency in purpose, and purer transparency of effects.

If Foucauldian thought insists that humanity must not forget the martial genealogy that accounts for the dispositions and proprieties which have come to be associated with it when lifted from the condition of war, so does it insist in near equal terms that life not surrender its immanent capacities to wage war in procreation and defence of its potentialities to outlive humanist constraints. In response to the resentful violence of liberal regimes its call to arms has been close to incessant. Throughout this book we have encountered different articulations of the ways in which life can and does recover its capacity to defend itself, develop counter-strategies, and defy the violence applied to it in its subjection to liberal regimes of governance. As liberal regimes have problematised life's undecidability as the source of the problem of war, and as the development of liberal peace has taken the form of a terrorisation of the very condition of being alive, each of the authors invoked here have as often tended to seek an answer in the return to and an insistence upon war as a necessary condition of possibility for the expression of life beyond the suffocating constraints of liberal modernity. Faced with the grand paradox of a liberal modernity in which the governing desire for a world devoid of violent differences forces life continually to choose sides, Foucauldian thought insists on the necessity that life always, ultimately, chooses itself and revolts. The martial bearings of liberal modernity revealed, the pursuit of a political response to the phenomenon of liberal terror has tended to assume the form of a war of resistance against the imposition of liberalism's insidious biometric violence. As such the political question which Foucauldian thought has repeatedly tried to invoke has been that of how to assume war as a condition of possibility for the constitution and generation of life. What form does life take when peace is no longer its precondition but its enemy? What form does life assume when war is the determinate condition of its possibility?

And yet the journey through the various dimensions of Foucauldian thought within which these questions have been sequentially posed is ultimately itself, also, a paradoxical one. Seeking other ways politically to construe the life of human being, ways which might compromise its seemingly endless polemologies and erstwhile resort to Terror, Foucauldian thought itself runs the risk of culminating in a form of biopolitical imperium where the question of what life is and what life may become is answered in accordance with the assertion of the necessity of the subjection of life to a time and space of war. In opposition to the attempts of liberal regimes to remove life from the condition of war, life itself is exhorted to embrace war as the condition in which it can recover its immanent tendencies and remove itself from the conditions of peace which liberal regimes attempt to enfold it within. In response to liberal regimes' attempts to pacify the life of societies biopolitically, each of these thinkers has sought an answer in the return to and an insistence upon war as a condition of possibility for the expression of resistance of life against its regimentation. Faced with the grand paradox of a modernity in which the promise of peace has always meant the targeting of rogue societies and subjectivities with the means of war and state terror, each of these thinkers have insisted on responding with their own wars of resistance and counter-strategies. The fundamental question that each of their theories turns on is that of how to assume war and strategy as a condition of possibility for the constitution and generation of resistance to a given regime of power.

In their different responses to this problem of how life resists the imposition of liberal strategies of pacification, I have sought to draw out the nuances and diversities in the accounts offered by Foucault, Deleuze and Guattari, Baudrillard, Virilio, and Negri. Foucault's seminal account of the martial origins of the tactics and strategies with which liberal regimes transform the polemical vitality of human being into logistical life has framed the narrative on which the account offered here hangs. Yet, as was discussed, when faced with the question of what life might otherwise become beyond its subjection to this military machine for the calculation of the infinite and the infinitesimal, Foucault's response proved more or less ineffable. The questions of how life might be understood to resist the tactics and strategies of liberal regimes, how it articulates a counter-conceptualisation of what form an alternative account of a life . worth living might take, and of how it goes about pursuing such an ideal, are difficult to answer from within the body of thought Foucault bequeathed us. It was in order to overcome these weaknesses that we turned to the rival accounts of the same dilemmas on offer in the works of the other authors engaged with in the book.

Throughout each of the other chapters we traced the idea of the existence of a different, subterranean war that rumbles away in the depths and interstices of liberal modernity. In the works of Deleuze and Guattari, Virilio, and Negri especially we encountered a faith in the idea that in spite of the breadth and depth of liberalism's machinery of subjection, life maintains the integrity of a knowledge and investment in an older, sometimes arcane, set of techniques for subversion, resistance, and defiance of power. Baudrillard's response tested the limits of the claim made here as to the shared commitment of these thinkers to the principle of being able to contest liberalism by founding an understanding of the human in its relation to a life lived in an alternative time and space of war. Yet although testing those limits in his attempt to construe the life of Terror outside of all polemological discourses, even Baudrillard's explanation for Terror remains within a particular kind of grid of intelligibility in which, akin to each of the authors addressed in this book, he attempts to locate Terror within the domain of the development of counter-strategies to liberal modernity. In spite of the significant differences in the formulations of responses to the questions of what human life is and what it may become, each of the authors that follows Foucault is suborned in one way or another to a counter-ontology of strategy and war. Against the soldierly life of uniformity and docility with which liberal regimes attempt to stamp their subjects in the name of liberal peace, Foucauldian thought has attempted to mobilise a war from within – a war conducted not simply in defence of an alternative account of life, but a war which embodies that alternative account of what life is.

We saw how this plays out in the thought of Deleuze and Guattari, where it is the nomadic tendency which defines life in its essence and makes possible all of human history and thought. It is this nomadic root to life which generates movements of human resistance to any attempts to territorialise the human. Thus, the role of Terror in a war against the codification of definitions of human life in international law as well as against the organisations, institutions, and practices which enforce such law, are, it can be argued, recuperations of the earlier historical movements of nomadic societies against sedentary civilisations. We saw likewise how Baudrillard offers an account of the root of life in the capacity for defiance; an obdurate defiance of all attempts to know what life is by protecting the obscurity of its truth, preserving its secret, refusing its revelation in human form by act of declaration or codification. Thus, Baudrillard argues, we discover in Terror the embodiment of such an account of life as defiance in a strategy based upon a principle of the refusal of the capacities for communication, negotiation, and all counter-subjective political practices. We saw in the development of the thought of Virilio an alternative account of life as an absolute tendency for mobility and circulation, and how his architectural practice has sought to reshape the urban spaces of the city to enable that account. How in turn his critique of the relative inhumanity of liberal city spaces can help to explain the targeting of the World Trade Center by Terror in 2001. And we saw in the works of Negri the attempt to develop an alternative account of life in terms of its absolute immanence, its refusal of transcendence, and how such an account of life can be used problematically to legitimate a form of resistance to liberalism which simultaneously refuses the strategies and tactics of terrorism.

Yet, ultimately, in the unravelling of this debate over war and the problems it poses for the political constitution of human life, it is still Foucault who maintains an ultimate significance. In contrast with the attempts of his peers to offer explanations for the ways in which life must search to recover its integrity in the idioms of war and counter-strategy, Foucault posed the problem of war and its relation to life in starkly different terms of a *problematisation*. The final question for Foucault was not that of how war can be waged by life in order to pursue alternative forms of politics, but how life might escape the limits of such a counter-strategic grid of intelligibility where the ideal of war remains the limit of its political and ethical horizons. How long, he asks in *Society Must Be Defended*, will it be until life itself recognises and is able to escape the limits of the invocations of these discourses of counter-strategy which other authors still insist on as an inexhaustible terrain? How long until life tires not so much of the old-fashioned demand for its neutrality but of these games of strategy, of proliferating divisions, minor offensives, sieges and snares, that enslaves it to the laws of war? Is there no idiom imaginable to life other than its endless subjection within strategic relations and incessant generation of war's limitless potentialities? Regardless of the challenges to the disciplinary techniques and biopolitical management for the manufacture of subjectivities that this insistence on exploring war's exteriority affords, Foucault insists that it is today as necessary to raise questions about the limits imposed on the potentialities for life when such an ontological account of being as time of war is mobilised as politics. If the peace that liberal regimes sanction and uphold is born out of a historically and politically contingent disequilibrium of force relations which negates life, then one means to contest that peace is to disturb its martial genealogy, to pervert its order and disinter its vital pathologies. Biopolitical life emerges in the context of this conflict as the residual forms which life assumes once liberal regimes quell its immanent potentiality. Forces of immanent war and liberal regimes of biopolitical production are situated in a relation of confrontation, but the development of liberal modernity has only ever functioned as the sign of the tragic struggle of immanence for its expression; not simply a sign of the impossibility of the fulfilment of liberal modernity but of the increased intensification and dissemination of the biopolitical imperium 'make war at all costs'. In attempting to valorise the temporality of war as a precondition for the salvation of life from its subjection to the biopolitical imperium, Foucauldian thought runs the risk of subjecting life to that same slavish imperium of biopolitics.

When will the endless duty of life to know itself better, expressed in the demand to return to that condition of war from whence it haplessly came, incite the challenge of a concept of living that exceeds such biopolitical imperia? This is the ultimate demand of Foucault to his peers. Those many and now long traditions of counter-opposing the imposition of peace by declaring it war, which are finding their culmination now in a multitude of 'dispersed and discontinuous' offensives, provide no substantial ground, he argues, from which to escape the dilemmas which the relations of war to life and liberal modernity pose for us. If we desire a resolution of the paradoxes which liberal modernity throws at us, and which are the crux of this contemporary global civil war over the political constitution of life, we may want to establish other ways of construing the life of human being, ones which compromise its seemingly endless polemologies and messianic yearnings for Terror.

References

Ali, T. (2003), 'Re-colonizing Iraq', *New Left Review* (21), pp. 1–19.

Alliez, E. (2004), *The Signature of the World: What is Deleuze and Guattari's Philosophy?* (Eliot Ross Albert and Alberto Toscano trans.) (New York and London, Continuum).

Alnasrawi, A. (2001), 'Iraq: Economic Sanctions and Consequences, 1990–2000', *Third World Quarterly* (vol. 22, no. 2), pp. 205–18.

Armitage, J. (2000), 'From Modernism to Hypermodernism and Beyond: An Interview with Paul Virilio' in John Armitage (ed.), *Paul Virilio: From Modernism to Hypermodernism and Beyond* (London, Sage), pp. 25–55.

Axworthy, L. (2001), 'Human Security and Global Governance', *Global Governance* (vol. 7, no. 1), pp. 19–23.

Barber, B. (2003), 'The War of All Against All: Terror and the Politics of Fear' in Verna V. Gehring (ed.), *War after September 11* (Oxford, Rowman & Littlefield), pp. 75–91.

Barkawi, T. (2006), *Globalization & War* (Oxford, Rowman & Littlefield).

Barkawi, T. and Laffey, M. (2002), 'Retrieving the Imperial: *Empire* and International Relations', *Millennium: Journal of International Studies* (vol. 31, no. 1), pp. 109–27.

_____ (ed.) (2001), *Democracy, Liberalism and War: Rethinking the Democratic Peace Debate* (Boulder, Lynne Rienner).

_____ (1999), 'The Imperial Peace: Democracy, Force and Globalization', *European Journal of International Relations* (vol. 5, no. 4), pp. 403–34.

Baudrillard, J. (2004), *Fragments* (Chris Turner trans.) (London and New York, Routledge).

_____ (2003), 'L-Esprit du Terrorisme' (Michel Valentin trans.) in Stanley Hauerwas and Frank Lentricchia (eds), *Dissent from the Homeland: Essays After September 11* (Durham and London, Duke University Press), pp. 149–61.

_____ (1999a), *The System of Objects* (James Benedict trans.) (London, Verso).

_____ (1999b), *The Consumer Society: Myths and Structures* (London, Sage).

_____ (1999c), *Symbolic Exchange and Death* (Iain Hamilton Grant trans.) (London, Sage).

_____ (1999d), *The Transparency of Evil* (London and New York, Verso).

_____ (1994), 'The Beaubourg Effect: Implosion and Deterrence' in Jean Baudrillard, *Simulacra and Simulation* (Sheila Faria Glaser trans.) (Ann Arbor, University of Michigan Press), pp. 61–73.

_____ (1991), *La Guerre du Golfe n'a Pas eu Lieu* (Paris, Galilée).

_____ (1990), *Fatal Strategies: Crystal Revenge* (Philip Beitchman and W.G.J.

Niesluchowski trans.) (New York, Semiotext).

_____ (1987), *Forget Foucault* (New York, Semiotext).

_____ (1983), *In the Shadow of the Silent Majorities, Or, The End of the Social and Other Essays* (Paul Foss, John Johnston and Paul Patton trans.) (New York, Semiotext).

_____ (1975), *The Mirror of Production* (Mark Poster trans.) (St. Louis, Telos Press).

Baudrillard, J. and Nouvel, J. (2002), *The Singular Objects of Architecture* (Robert Bononno trans.) (Minneapolis and London, University of Minnesota Press).

Berman, M. (2002), 'When Bad Buildings Happen to Good People' in Michael Sorkin and Sharon Zukin (eds), *After the World Trade Center: Rethinking New York City* (New York and London, Routledge), pp. 1–12.

Berman, P. (2003), *Terror and Liberalism* (New York and London, Norton).

bin Laden, O. (2001), Untitled Speech (Doha, Qatar, Al Jazeera TV, October 7).

Black, J. (2004), *War and the New Disorder in the 21st Century* (London and New York, Continuum).

Bleier, R. (2002), 'Invading Iraq: The Road to Perpetual War', *Middle East Policy* (vol. IX, no. 4), pp. 35–42.

Bobbitt, P. (2003), *The Shield of Achilles: War, Peace and the Course of History* (London, Penguin).

Boron, A.O. (2005), *Empire & Imperialism: A Critical Reading of Michael Hardt and Antonio Negri* (Jessica Cassiro trans.) (London and New York, Zed Books).

Brown, C. (2002), 'Narratives of Religion, Civilization and Modernity' in Ken Booth and Tim Dunne (eds), *Worlds in Collision: Terror and the Future of Global Order* (Basingstoke, Palgrave), pp. 293–302.

Bush, G.W. (2002), 'Message to the Congress of the United States', www .whitehouse.gov/news/releases/2001/09/20010929.html.

_____ (2001a), 'Address to a Joint Session of Congress and the American People', United States Capitol, Washington D.C., www.whitehouse .gov/news/releases/2001/09/20010920–8.html.

_____ (2001b), 'Radio Address of the President to the Nation', www.white-house.fed.us/news/releases/2001/09/20010929.html.

Butler, J. (2004), *Precarious Life: The Powers of Mourning and Violence* (London and New York, Verso).

_____ (1999), *Subjects of Desire: Hegelian Reflections in Twentieth-Century France* (New York, Columbia University Press).

_____ (1997), *The Psychic Life of Power: Theories in Subjection* (Stanford, Stanford University Press).

Butler, R. (1999), *Jean Baudrillard: The Defence of the Real* (London, Sage).

Callinicos, A. (2002), 'The Actuality of Imperialism', *Millennium: Journal of*

International Studies (vol. 31, no. 2), pp. 319–26.

Campbell, D. (1998), *Writing Security: United States Foreign Policy and the Politics of Identity* (Manchester and New York, Manchester University Press).

Campbell, D. and Honigsbaum, M. (2005), 'Fatal Mistakes That Cost De Menezes His Life', *The Guardian* (18/8).

Castells, M. (1997), *The Power of Identity* (Oxford, Blackwell).

____ (1996), *The Rise of the Network Society* (Oxford, Blackwell).

Chandler, D. (2002), *From Kosovo to Kabul: Human Rights and International Intervention* (London, Pluto).

Clausewitz, C.V. (1993), *On War* (Michael Howard and Peter Paret trans.) (London, Everyman).

Cole, D. (2003), *Enemy Aliens: Double Standards and Constitutional Freedoms in the War on Terrorism* (New York and London, New Press).

Cook, D. (1995), 'Symbolic Exchange in Hyperreality' in Douglas Kellner (ed.), *Baudrillard: A Critical Reader* (Oxford, Basil Blackwell), pp. 150–67.

Coward, M. (2004), 'Urbicide in Bosnia' in Stephen Graham (ed.), *Cities, War and Terrorism: Towards an Urban Geopolitics* (Oxford, Blackwell), pp. 154–71.

____ (2002), 'Community as Heterogeneous Ensemble: Mostar and Multiculturalism', *Alternatives* (27), pp. 29–66.

Cox, M. (2003), 'The Empire's Back in Town or America's Imperial Temptation – Again', *Millennium: Journal of International Studies* (vol. 32, no. 1), pp. 1–27.

Cronin, A.K. (2002), 'Rethinking Sovereignty: American Strategy in the Age of Terrorism', *Survival* (vol. 44, no. 2), pp. 119–39.

Cruikshank, B. (1999), *The Will to Empower: Democratic Citizens and Other Subjects* (New York, Cornell University Press).

Dandeker, C. (1990), *Surveillance, Power & Modernity* (Cambridge and Oxford, Polity Press).

Darton, E. (2002), 'The Janus Face of Architectural Terrorism: Minoru Yamasaki, Mohammed Atta, and Our World Trade Center' in Michael Sorkin and Sharon Zukin (eds), *After the World Trade Center: Rethinking New York City* (New York and London, Routledge), pp. 87–95.

Dean. M. (1999), *Governmentality: Power and Rule in Modern Society* (London, Sage).

Deleuze, G. and Guattari, F. (2000), *Anti-Oedipus: Capitalism & Schizophrenia* (Robert Hurley, Mark Seem and Helen R. Lane trans.) (London, Athlone Press).

____ (1999), *A Thousand Plateaus: Capitalism & Schizophrenia* (Brian Massumi trans.) (London, Athlone Press).

____ (1996), *What is Philosophy?* (Graham Burchell and Hugh Tomlinson trans.) (London, Verso).

References

Department of Homeland Security (2004), *The National Plan for Research and Development in Support of Critical Infrastructure Protection*, www.dhs.gov /interweb/assetlibrary/ST_2004_NCIP_RD_PlanFINALApr05.pdf.

____ (2001), *Are You Ready?* www.fema.gov/areyouready/.

Der Derian, J. (2001), *Virtuous War: Mapping the Military-Industrial-Media-Entertainment Network* (Boulder and Oxford, Westview Press).

____ (ed.) (1998), *The Virilio Reader* (Oxford, Blackwell).

____ (1995), 'Simulation: The Highest Stage of Capitalism?' in Douglas Kellner (ed.), *Baudrillard: A Critical Reader* (Oxford, Basil Blackwell), pp. 189–207.

Dillon, M. (1996), *Politics of Security: Toward a Political Philosophy of Continental Thought* (London, Routledge).

____ (1990), 'The Alliance of Security and Subjectivity', *Current Research on Peace and Violence* (vol. 13, no. 3), pp. 101–24.

____ (1989), 'Modernity, Discourse and Deterrence', *Current Research on Peace and Violence* (vol. XII, no. 2), pp. 90–104.

Dillon, M. and Reid, J. (2001), 'Global Liberal Governance: Biopolitics, Security and War', *Millennium: Journal of International Studies* (vol. 30, no. 1), pp. 41–66.

____ (2000), 'Global Governance, Liberal Peace and Complex Emergency', *Alternatives* (vol. 25, no. 1), pp. 115–43.

Douglas, I. (1996), 'The Calm Before the Storm: Virilio's Debt to Foucault and Some Notes on Contemporary Global Capital', *Speed* (vol. 1, no. 4).

Doyle, M. (1997), *Ways of War and Peace* (New York and London, Norton & Company).

____ (1986), 'Liberalism and World Politics', *American Political Science Review* (vol. 80, no. 4), pp. 1151–69.

____ (1983), 'Kant, Liberal Legacies, and Foreign Affairs', Parts 1 and 2, *Philosophy and Public Affairs* (vol. 12, nos. 3–4), pp. 205–54, 323–53.

Duffield, M. (2001), *Global Governance and the New Wars: The Merging of Development & Security* (London and New York, Zed Books).

Dunn, D.H. (2003), 'Myths, Motivations and "Misunderestimations": The Bush Administration and Iraq', *International Affairs* (vol. 79, no. 2), pp. 279–97.

Edkins, J. (1999), *Poststructuralism and International Relations: Bringing the Political Back In* (Boulder and London, Lynne Rienner).

Eland, I. (2002), 'The Empire Strikes Out: The "New Imperialism" and Its Fatal Flaws', *Policy Analysis* (459), pp. 1–27.

Elshtain, J.B. (2004), *Just War Against Terror: The Burden of American Power in a Violent World* (New York, Basic Books).

Eysenck, H.J. (1968), 'Humanism and the Future' in A.J.Ayer (ed.), *The Humanist Outlook* (London, Pemberton Publishing), pp. 265–77.

Fanon, F. (1986), *Black Skins, White Masks* (Charles Lam Markmann trans.) (London, Pluto).

Foucault, M. (2003), *Society Must Be Defended: Lectures at the Collège de France 1975–76* (David Macey trans.) (London, Picador).

____ (2001a), 'Governmentality' in Michel Foucault, *Power* (James D. Faubion ed.) (Robert Hurley trans.) (London, Allen Lane), pp. 201–22.

____ (2001b), 'The Subject and Power' in Michel Foucault, *Power* (James D. Faubion ed.) (Robert Hurley trans.) (London, Allen Lane), pp. 326–48.

____ (2001c), 'Confronting Governments: Human Rights' in Michel Foucault, *Power* (James D. Faubion ed.) (Robert Hurley trans.) (London, Allen Lane), pp. 474–5.

____ (1997a), 'Structuralism and Post-Structuralism' in Michel Foucault, *Ethics* (Paul Rabinow ed.) (Robert Hurley trans.) (London, Allen Lane), pp. 437–48.

____ (1997b), 'Security, Territory, Population' in Michel Foucault, *Ethics* (Paul Rabinow ed.) (Robert Hurley trans.) (London, Allen Lane), pp. 67–71.

____ (1992), *The Use of Pleasure: The History of Sexuality 2* (Robert Hurley trans.) (London, Penguin).

____ (1991), *Discipline and Punish: The Birth of the Prison* (Alan Sheridan trans.) (London, Penguin).

____ (1990), *The History of Sexuality: Volume One, An Introduction* (Robert Hurley trans.) (London, Penguin).

Freedman, L. (2002), 'The Coming War on Terrorism' in Lawrence Freedman (ed.), *Superterrorism: Policy Responses* (Oxford, Blackwell), pp. 40–56.

Fukuyama, F. (2002), 'History and September 11' in Ken Booth and Tim Dunne (eds), *Worlds in Collision: Terror and the Future of Global Order* (Basingstoke, Palgrave), pp. 27–36.

____ (1992), *The End of History and the Last Man* (New York, Free Press).

Gabardi, W. (2001), *Negotiating Postmodernism* (Minneapolis and London, University of Minnesota Press).

Gane, M. (2000), *Jean Baudrillard: In Radical Uncertainty* (London, Pluto).

Gearson, J. (2002), 'The Nature of Modern Terrorism' in Lawrence Freedman (ed.), *Superterrorism: Policy Responses* (Oxford, Blackwell), pp. 7–24.

Genosko, G. (1994), *Baudrillard and Signs: Signification Ablaze* (London and New York, Routledge).

Giddens, A. (2002), *The Nation-State and Violence: Volume Two of A Contemporary Critique of Historical Materialism* (Oxford, Polity).

Gill, S. (2000), 'Toward a Postmodern Prince? The Battle in Seattle as a Moment in the New Politics of Globalization', *Millennium: Journal of International Studies* (vol. 29, no. 1), pp. 131–40.

Gilroy, P. (2004), *After Empire: Melancholia or Convivial Culture?* (London, Routledge).

Gray, C. (1999), *Modern Strategy* (Oxford, Oxford University Press).

Halperin, S. (2004), *War and Social Change in Modern Europe: The Great*

References

Transformation Revisited (Cambridge, Cambridge University Press).

Hardt, M. and Negri, A. (2004), *Multitude: War and Democracy in the Age of Empire* (New York, Penguin Press).

_____ (2001), *Empire* (Cambridge, Massachusetts, and London, Harvard University Press).

Harvey, D. (2002), 'Cracks in the Edifice of the Empire State' in Michael Sorkin and Sharon Zukin (eds), *After the World Trade Center: Rethinking New York City* (New York and London, Routledge), pp. 57–67.

Hegarty, P. (2004), *Jean Baudrillard: Live Theory* (London and New York, Continuum).

Hirst, P. (2001), *War and Power in the 21st Century* (Cambridge, Polity).

Hobbes, T. (1985), *Leviathan* (London, Penguin).

Holland, E. (1999), *Deleuze and Guattari's Anti-Oedipus: Introduction to Schizoanalysis* (London and New York, Routledge).

Holsti, K.J. (2001), *The State, War, and the State of War* (Cambridge, Cambridge University Press).

Honderich, T. (1976), *Three Essays on Political Violence* (Oxford, Blackwell).

Hutchings, K. (1999), *International Political Theory: Rethinking Ethics in a Global Era* (London, Sage).

Ignatieff, M. (2001), *Virtual War: Kosovo and Beyond* (London, Vintage).

Ikenberry, G.J. (2002), 'America's Imperial Ambition', *Foreign Affairs* (September–October), pp. 44–60.

Jabri, V. (2005), 'Critical Theory and Political Agency in Time of War', *International Relations* (vol. 19, no. 1), pp. 70–8.

Jormakka, K. (2002), *Flying Dutchmen: Motion in Architecture* (Basel, Birkhäuser).

Kagan, R. (2002), 'Power and Weakness', *Policy Review* (113), available at www.policyreview.org/Jun02/kagan.html.

Kaldor, M. (2003), *Global Civil Society: An Answer to War* (Oxford, Polity).

_____ (2002), *Old and New Wars* (Oxford, Polity).

Kant, I. (1983), *Perpetual Peace* (Indianapolis, Hackett).

_____ (1964), *Critique of Pure Reason* (J.M.D. Meikleson trans.) (London and New York, Everyman).

Kellner, D. (2002), 'September 11, Social Theory and Democratic Politics', *Theory, Culture & Society* (vol. 19, no. 4), pp. 147–59.

_____ (2000), 'Virilio, War and Technology: Some Critical Reflections' in John Armitage (ed.), *Paul Virilio: From Modernism to Hypermodernism and Beyond* (London, Sage), pp. 103–25.

_____ (1995), 'Introduction – Baudrillard in the Fin-de-Millennium' in Douglas Kellner (ed.), *Baudrillard: A Critical Reader* (Oxford, Basil Blackwell), pp. 1–23.

Kennelly, D. (2003), 'Q&A With ... Thomas P.M. Barnett', *Doublethink*

(Summer Issue), pp. 17–21.

Krause, K. and Williams, M.J. (eds) (1996), *Critical Security Studies: Concepts and Cases* (London, University College London Press).

King, G. and Murray, C. (2001–2002), 'Rethinking Human Security', *Political Science Quarterly* (vol. 116, no. 4), pp. 585–610.

Kistner, U. (2004), 'Raison D'Etat: Philosophy of and Against the State', *Interventions* (vol. 6, no. 2), pp. 242–51.

Laclau, E. and Mouffe, C. (1985), *Hegemony & Socialist Strategy: Towards a Radical Democratic Politics* (London, Verso).

Leach, N. (2000), 'Virilio and Architecture' in John Armitage (ed.), *Paul Virilio: From Modernism to Hypermodernism and Beyond* (London, Sage), pp. 71–84.

Levy, J.S. (1988), 'Domestic Politics and War', *Journal of Interdisciplinary History* (18), pp. 653–73.

Liebeskind, D. (1997), 'Traces of the Unborn' in Paul Virilio and Claude Parent, *Architecture Principe: 1966 and 1996* (George Collins trans.) (Besançon, France, Les Éditions de L'Imprimeur), pp. 157–9.

Lipschutz, R. (ed.) (1995), *On Security* (New York, Columbia University Press).

Lozano-Hamer, R. (2002), 'Alien Relationships from Public Space' in V2_Publishing, *Transurbanism* (Rotterdam, RAI), pp. 139–59.

Lynne Doty, R. (1999), 'Racism, Desire, and the Politics of Immigration', *Millennium: Journal of International Studies* (vol. 28, no. 3), pp. 585–606.

MacGinty, R. (2003), 'The Pre-war Reconstruction of Iraq', *Third World Quarterly* (vol. 24, no. 4), pp. 601–17.

Macmillan, J. (1998), *On Liberal Peace: Democracy, War and the International Order* (London, Tauris).

Malanczuk, P. (1991), 'The Kurdish Crisis and Allied Intervention in the Aftermath of the Second Gulf War', *European Journal of International Law* (2), pp. 114–32.

Mandeville, B. (1962), *The Fable of the Bees, Or, Private Vices, Publick Benefits* (London, Capricorn).

Marchand, M., Reid, J. and Berents, B. (1998) 'Migration (Im-)Mobility, and Modernity: Toward a Feminist Understanding of the Global Prostitution Scene', *Millennium: Journal of International Studies* (vol. 27, no. 4), pp. 955–81.

Marks, J. (1998), *Gilles Deleuze: Vitalism and Multiplicity* (London, Pluto Press).

Marx, K. (1988), *The Communist Manifesto* (New York and London, Norton).

Massumi, B. (1999), *A User's Guide to Capitalism and Schizophrenia: Deviations from Deleuze and Guattari* (Cambridge, MA, and London, Massachusetts Institute of Technology Press).

Maturana, H. and Varela, F. (1980), *Autopoiesis and Cognition: The Realization of the Living* (Dordrecht, D. Reidel).

McRae, R. and Hubert, D. (2001), *Human Security and the New Diplomacy:*

References

Protecting People, Promoting Peace (Montreal, McGill-Queen's University Press).

Messner, D. and Nuscheler, F. (2002), 'World Politics – Structures and Trends' in Paul Kennedy, Dirk Messner and Frank Nuscheler (eds), *Global Trends & Global Governance* (London, Pluto Press), pp. 125–55.

Mulder, A. (2002), 'Transurbanism' in V2_Publishing, *Transurbanism* (Rotterdam, RAI), pp. 5–15.

Negri, A. (2005), *The Politics of Subversion: A Manifesto for the Twenty-First Century* (James Newell trans.) (Cambridge and Malden, Polity Press).

_____ (2004), *Subversive Spinoza: (Un)Contemporary Variations* (Timothy S. Murphy ed.) (Timothy S. Murphy, Michael Hardt, Ted Stolze, and Charles T. Wolfe trans.) (Manchester and New York, Manchester University Press).

_____ (2003), *Time for Revolution* (Matteo Mandarini trans.) (London, Verso).

_____ (1991), *The Savage Anomaly: The Power of Spinoza's Metaphysics and Politics* (Michael Hardt trans.) (Minneapolis and Oxford, University of Minnesota Press).

Negri, A. with Dufourmantelle, A. (2004), *Negri on Negri: Antonio Negri in Conversation with Anne Dufourmantelle* (M.B. DeBevoise trans.) (New York and London, Routledge).

Norris, C. (2000a), *Deconstruction and the 'Unfinished Project of Modernity'* (London, Athlone Press).

_____ (2000b), *Deconstruction: Theory and Practice* (London and New York, Routledge).

Nye, J.S. and Owens, W. (1996), 'America's Information Edge', *Foreign Affairs* (March/April), pp. 20–36.

Parent, P. (1997), 'Potentialism' in Paul Virilio and Claude Parent, *Architecture Principe: 1966 and 1996* (George Collins trans.) (Besançon, France, Les Éditions de L'Imprimeur), pp. VIII–IX.

Patton, P. (2000), *Deleuze & the Political* (London and New York, Routledge).

Peukert, D. (1989), *Inside Nazi Germany* (Harmondsworth, Penguin).

Philo, C. (2000), 'Foucault's Geography' in Mike Crang and Nigel Thrift (eds), *Thinking Space* (London and New York, Routledge), pp. 205–38.

Pick, D. (1993), *War Machine: The Rationalisation of Slaughter in the Modern Age* (New Haven and London, Yale University Press).

Rawls, J. (1980), 'Kantian Constructivism in Moral Theory', *The Journal of Philosophy* (88), pp. 515–72.

Redhead, S. (2004), *Paul Virilio: Theorist for an Accelerated Culture* (Edinburgh, Edinburgh University Press).

Reid, J. (2003a), 'Deleuze's War Machine: Nomadism Against the State', *Millennium: Journal of International Studies* (vol. 32, no. 1), pp. 57–85.

_____ (2003b), 'Foucault on Clausewitz: Conceptualizing the Relationship Between War and Power', *Alternatives* (vol. 28, no. 1), pp. 1–28.

Roberts, A. (2003), 'Law and the Use of Force after Iraq', *Survival* (vol. 45, no. 2), pp. 31–56.

Rose, N. (1999a), *Powers of Freedom: Reframing Political Thought* (Cambridge, Cambridge University Press).

_____ (1999b), *Governing the Soul: The Shaping of the Private Self* (London and New York, Free Association Books).

_____ (1993), 'Government, Authority and Expertise in Advanced Liberalism', *Economy & Society* (vol. 22, no. 3), pp. 283–99.

Russett, B. (1993), *Grasping the Democratic Peace* (Princeton, Princeton University Press).

Ruthven, M. (2004), *A Fury for God: The Islamist Attack on America* (London, Granta).

Shapiro, M.J. (2004), 'Constructing "America": Architectural Thought-Worlds', *Theory & Event* (vol. 7, no. 4).

_____ (2001), 'Sounds of Nationhood', *Millennium: Journal of International Studies* (vol. 30, no. 3), pp. 584–601.

Shaw, M. (2005), *The New Western Way of War* (Oxford, Polity)

_____ (2004), 'New Wars of the City: Relationships of "Urbicide" and "Genocide" in Stephen Graham (ed.), *Cities, War and Terrorism: Toward an Urban Geopolitics* (Oxford, Blackwell), pp. 141–53.

_____ (2003), *War & Genocide* (Oxford, Polity)

_____ (2002), 'Post-Imperial and Quasi-Imperial: State and Empire in the Global Era', *Millennium: Journal of International Studies* (vol. 31, no. 2), pp. 327–36.

Simons, J. (1995), *Foucault & the Political* (London, Routledge).

Spuybroek, L. (2002), 'The Structure of Vagueness' in V2_Publishing, *Transurbanism* (Rotterdam, NAI), pp. 65–87.

Taylor, C. (1986), 'Foucault on Freedom and Truth' in David Hoy (ed.), *Foucault: A Political Reader* (Oxford, Blackwell).

United Nations (2005a), Office of the Iraq Programme, Oil for Food, 'Fact Sheet', available at www.un.org/Depts/oip/background/fact-sheet.html.

_____ (2005b), United Nations Security Council Resolutions, Resolution 1483 (2003), www.un.org/Docs/sc/unsc_resolutions03.html.

V2_Publishing (2002), *Transurbanism* (Rotterdam, NAI).

Virilio, P. (2002), *Ground Zero* (Chris Turner trans.) (London and New York, Verso).

_____ (1997), 'Disorientation' in Paul Virilio and Claude Parent, *Architecture Principe: 1966 and 1996* (George Collins trans.) (Besançon, France, Les Éditions de L'Imprimeur), pp. 7–13.

_____ (1990), *Popular Defense & Ecological Struggles* (Mark Polizzotti trans.) (New York, Semiotext).

_____ (1986), *Speed and Politics* (Mark Polizzotti trans.) (New York, Semiotext).

Virilio, P. and Lotringer, S. (2002), *Crepescular Dawn* (Mike Taormina trans.)

References

(New York, Semiotext).

____ (1997), *Pure War* (Mark Polizzotti trans.) (New York, Semiotext).

____ (1997b), 'Manhattan Out' in Paul Virilio and Claude Parent, *Architecture Principe: 1966 and 1996* (George Collins trans.) (Besançon, France, Les Éditions de L'Imprimeur), pp. V–VI.

Virilio, P. and Parent, C. (1997), 'The Oblique Function' in Paul Virilio and Claude Parent, *Architecture Principe: 1966 and 1996* (George Collins trans.) (Besançon, France, Les Éditions de L'Imprimeur), pp. III–V.

____ (1997b), 'The Third Urban Order' in Paul Virilio and Claude Parent, *Architecture Principe: 1966 and 1996* (George Collins trans.) (Besançon, France, Les Éditions de L'Imprimeur), pp. VI–VIII.

Vitruvius (1960), *The Ten Books of Architecture* (Morris Hicky Morgan trans.) (New York, Dover Publications).

Walker, R.B.J. (2002), 'On the Immanence/Imminence of *Empire*', *Millennium: Journal of International Studies* (vol. 31, no. 2), pp. 337–45.

Walt, S. (1991), 'The Renaissance of Security Studies', *International Studies Quarterly* (vol. 35, no. 2), pp. 211–39.

Welter, V.M. (2002), *Biopolis: Patrick Geddes and the City of Life* (Cambridge, Massachusetts, and London, Massachusetts Institute of Technology Press).

Wigley, M. (2002a), 'Insecurity by Design' in Michael Sorkin and Sharon Zukin (eds), *After the World Trade Center: Rethinking New York City* (London and New York, Routledge), pp. 69–85.

____ (2002b), 'Resisting the City' in V2_Publishing, *Transurbanism* (Rotterdam, RAI), pp. 103–21.

Wood, E.M. (2005), *Empire of Capital* (London, Verso).

Wyn Jones, R. (1999), *Security, Strategy and Critical Theory* (Boulder, Lynne Rienner).

Yaphe, J.S. (2003), 'America's War on Iraq: Myths and Opportunities', *Adelphi Papers* (vol. 354, no. 1), pp. 23–44.

Žižek, S. (2003), 'Welcome to the Desert of the Real!' in Stanley Hauerwas and Frank Lentricchia (eds), *Dissent from the Homeland: Essays after September 11* (Durham and London, Duke University Press), pp. 131–5.

____ (2000), *The Ticklish Subject: The Absent Centre of Political Ontology* (London and New York, Verso).

Zolo, D. (2002), *Invoking Humanity: War, Law and Global Order* (London and New York, Continuum).

Index

Index

identity politics 68–9
Ignatieff, Michael 55
imperialism 41–2, 62, 74, 79
   the United States 50–1, 53–5, 74
Independence Day 77
International Committee of the Red Cross
   58
International Relations theory 3, 12, 15,
   22, 56
   post-structuralism 7
   War on Terror 48, 51
   World Trade Center attack 91
Iran 31
Iraq 10, 19, 41, 48, 53–6
Islam 72–4, 92

Kaldor, Mary 7, 60, 75, 82
Kant, Immanuel 1, 2, 3, 18, 107, 109
Kellner, Douglas 60
Koolhas, Rem 90

liberal extremism 81
liberal humanitarianism 4–6, 48, 53–5, 58
liberal international theory 3, 12, 20, 40,
   49-51, 60
liberal modernity x, 1–3, 16, 17–18, 20,
   27, 45, 47, 52, 62, 79, 81, 82–3, 86–7,
   95, 99-101, 102, 105–107, 111, 116,
   123, 125–26, 128
liberal peace 2–3, 5
liberal regimes ix–x, 10–12, 16, 18–26, 40,
   43–6, 60–1, 64, 66, 73, 78–9, 82–3,
   86, 88, 94–5, 100, 103–107, 110,
   113–114, 116, 125–126
   modernity 86–7, 121
   biopolitics of 5–6, 29-35, 38, 75–6
   existing critiques of 4–6, 124
   globalisation of 67–8, 118–120
   illiberalism of 78
   strategies of 4–5, 63–4, 67–70, 75–6, 81,
     95, 109, 112, 120
liberal societies 1, 6, 17–19, 27, 34–6, 40,
   44, 47, 60, 77–8, 86–7, 93, 99-101,
   102–104, 106–107, 113, 119-120, 122
Liebeskind, Daniel 96
life sciences 36
logistical life 13–16, 18–22, 33–9, 43–5,
   63–4, 102, 120, 122–123, 126

logistical order 30–2
logistical strategies 33, 35, 37, 43–4, 49,
   123
Lotringer, Sylvère 99
Lozano-Hemmer, Raphael 98

Mandeville, Bernard 70
Marx, Karl 5
Marxism 41, 51, 103
Maturana, Humberto 98
Menezes, Jean Charles de 38
military sciences 20, 22–7, 34–6
Mill, John Stuart 70
Montaigne, Michel de 79
Moro, Aldo 106
Mulder, Arjen 98
multi-culturalism 68

nation-states 67–8
National Common Operating Picture for
   Critical Infrastructure 37
National Infrastructure Protection Plan
   34
National Plan for Research and
   Development in Support of Critical
   Infrastructure Protection 35–7
Nazism 29-30, 119
Negri, Antonio 15, 39, 57, 101, 102–104,
   126, 127
   biopolitical production 104–106
   concept of biopolitics 117–118
   democratic violence 104–107, 119-122
   politics of resistance 102–103
   involvement with Red Brigades 106
   on global wars of resistance 115
   on the polemical being of the
     multitude 106–111, 114–118, 122
Neo-Gramscian Theories of
   International Relations 41, 115
New York 85, 93
Nietzsche, Friedrich 80
nomadic life 13–14, 39, 44–7, 57, 59, 63,
   70, 76, 94, 102
nomadism 43–4, 46, 47, 91, 105, 127
   distinction from migration 46
   relation with cities 97
non-governmental organisations 51, 54–7
Norris, Christopher 80–1

[*143*]